Spiritual Maturity

God's Will for
Emotional Health
and Healing

Cresenda Jones

About the author:

Cresenda Jones, a certified life coach, has been a disciple of Christ since 1985 in the Charlotte, North Carolina; Athens and Atlanta, Georgia; Philadelphia, Pennsylvania, and New Jersey churches of Christ. She moved to South Florida in 2013. As a result of her experiences and professional responsibilities, she became interested in personal growth (mental health and emotional maturity). She has received professional counseling since 2001 and has read countless books on those subjects. She has earned two master's degrees (MBA—LaSalle University;  M.Ed.—University of Georgia) and expects to obtain her license as a mental health counselor in 2016.

Cresenda has worked as a school principal and district mathematics and science supervisor. She has facilitated nine group discussions using David Seamands' *Healing for Damaged Emotions Workbook*. The first group discussion was in Philadelphia, with subsequent discussions in South Jersey, Newark, Brooklyn, the Bronx, Central New Jersey, and now three groups in South Florida.

You can reach Cresenda at **cresenda@cresendajones.com**.

JOY Publishing
P. O. Box 880484
Boca Raton, FL 33488-0484

TABLE OF CONTENTS

ACKNOWLEDGEMENTS

Most of all, I appreciate and thank God, the giver of all grace, hope, wisdom, knowledge, and growth. With God, all things are possible! Apart from God, I can do nothing (John 15:5).

Secondly, no words could ever thank Cynthia "Syntcha" Darby, Kelly Reilly Baldwin, Kareema Gray, 43

PhD, Jacquelyn Windle-Thompson, Hélène Mbangu, Simone Bell, and Fabiola Toney who read, edited, and contributed to this book. Thank you all for your love for me and faith in me!

A special thanks also goes out to those who encouraged me, read the manuscript, or provided feedback: Beverly Polite, Theresa Clark, Wendy Bartlett O'Briant, Tracy Gibson Barlow, Rosalind Kimbrough McFadden, Kudzai Dombo, Clio Hamilton Austin, Tasha Bagley, Dennis Fiandra, Paulette Blowe, Sherrie Hart, Robyn Thibodeaux, Carla Channell Ruiz, Nathalie Pilar, Ann Sullivan, Karesse Lockhard, Joey Harris, Randy Ainsworth, Karlton Roberts, Thomo Cobo, Francis Antoine, the Simmons family (dog pound), Steve Fuller, Linda Close, Paul Vasquez, Ramona Fryson, Senja Hedman Sanchez, Amy Morgan, and Gina Poirier. I can't explain the comfort in knowing that if I ever need anything, I can ask and not feel like a burden. Thank you!

I also wish to thank those who have served in the churches and ministries of which I have been a part: James and Kim Campbell, Perry and Debra Cox, Bernie (dec) and Martha Alspaugh, Cheryl (dec) and Ricky Mann, Don and Heidi Burroughs, Johnny and Glorimar Rivera, Uche Azuakoemu Amudipe, Kevin and Trecina Holland, John Churchville, Wil Workman, and Heather Seachrist Geeting. You all have sacrificed so that others can have a relationship with God and the life "to the full" he has planned for each of us. Thank you, thank you, thank you!

Thanks also to my family members Vernon Jones (dec), Joyce Siler, Carmen Jones, Michael Siler, Mary Bowie, and Charles and Angelyn Crumbley who have given their best.

A special thanks to Vicki Jacoby who exhibited great interest in this subject which, I believe, is the "missing link" for many disciples in their growth efforts.

Lastly, I want to thank my heroes and partners in personal, character, and emotional growth. The *Healing for Damaged Emotions Workbook* discussion group participants in Philadelphia, South Jersey, Central Jersey, North Jersey, the Bronx, Brooklyn, Miami, and Palm Beach are my heroes. These women pushed past their fears to deal with heart and soul issues. Such a journey takes authentic courage. You all have given me wind for my wings!

DEDICATION

*This book is dedicated to the spiritual women who have
known me the longest, encouraged my soul the most,
and helped me grow from the inside out—in my heart and
soul. Thank you, Joyce Siler, Kimula Campbell, and Asha
George-Guiser for your love, faith, zeal, perseverance, and
inspirational example. You have poured into me and thus
made this book possible. My prayer is that through this
book, I will be able to pass on some of the richness that I
have been given in you.*

Foreword

A well-known Bible passage from both the testaments instructs us how to love God, but what does it mean to "love the Lord your God with all your heart and with all your soul and with all your strength and with all your mind"? (Deuteronomy 6:5, Luke 10:27). How does this type of love show in our lives? So much of what transpires during our formative years affects our perception and understanding about the nature of God and can hinder us from loving him wholeheartedly.

This is a book that can help us understand the hurts and traumas from our past, by means of a guided discovery to clear away the debris. Each chapter contains points and places for reflection, requiring a personal response after digging into the Scriptures. Readers are gently nudged along and coached by Cresenda Jones' wise words of encouragement, so that we may see closure to the difficulties facing us.

There are many self-help books on the market today, but where can believers find a clear book that is not focused just on "self," but on our lives in relation to God? By shoring up our spiritual foundations and facing the madness surrounding our lives, we can learn to connect to our Father and love him with our heart, soul, strength, and mind. As *The Message* version puts it: "Love the Lord your God with all your passion and prayer and muscle and intelligence." And Cresenda's book will help you do just that.

—Vicki Jacoby
Christian teacher and international speaker

Introduction

If someone claims, "I know him well!" but doesn't keep his commandments, he's obviously a liar. His life doesn't match his words. *But the one who keeps God's word is the person in whom we see God's mature love.* This is the only way to be sure we're in God. Anyone who claims to be intimate with God ought to live the same kind of life Jesus lived (1 John 2:4–6 MSG, emphasis added).

God has the most amazing plans for each of us here on earth. Not only does he want us to live life, but he has planned for us to enjoy life "to the full" (John 10:10). God has also called us to love him with all of our heart, soul, mind, and strength (Mark 12:30). He has called us to grow past spiritual infancy to spiritual maturity.

For most of us, the easier part of the challenge is to love God with all of our mind and strength. If we put our mind to it, we may be able to change outside and surface behaviors without really changing the heart and soul. Yet, in Ephesians 4:12–14, God calls us to grow and become mature, attaining to the whole measure of the fullness of Christ. In Philippians he calls us to live up to what we've attained (Philippians 3:16). He knows that it's best for us to present each other fully mature in Christ (Colossians 1:27–29). God wants what we want: to see us reach a level of maturity that will allow us to distinguish good from evil (Hebrews 5:14). He has even planned for us to be "mature and complete, not lacking anything" (James 1:4). Though I worked extremely hard to be the best disciple of Christ I could be, I had no idea how important it was to address the God-given emotional aspects of my being. I didn't know it, but my emotions were impacting every area of my life. Since I wasn't intentionally aware of and managing my emotions, they were managing me!

Most of us have worked for as long as we've been disciples of Jesus on being all that we can be spiritually. But until we address the heart and soul love that God calls us to, we will not attain to the maturity that God desires for our lives and we will miss out on the incredible gift of living his "life to the full." Some of us have opted out of the hard work required to become emotionally intelligent and mature. As a result, we've paid the price many times over for this neglect. Our personal well-being, peace, and serenity and our emotional intelligence (self-knowledge, self-management, social awareness, and relationship management skills) have all suffered because we are not all that Jesus was as he "matured, growing up in both body and spirit" (Luke 2:51–52 MSG). When we expect to live life to the full without dealing with our emotions, we are building with hay or straw and will be disappointed (1 Corinthians 3:12–15). **Without emotional intelligence and personal growth, our lives will be like the seed that fell among thorns** (Luke 8:14). **We will not be able to most effectively or spiritually handle life's worries, riches, and pleasures, and we will not mature.**

One of my all-time favorite quotes is, "Insanity is doing the same thing over and over again and expecting different results." We can stop the madness if we are willing to address heart and soul issues. The insane thinking is when we believe that we can have the most amazing chocolate cake without all the required ingredients: desiring and expecting God's life to the full when we don't give attention to character growth and emotional maturity. It's madness to think that we can be all that God has planned for us without keeping a firm grasp on both our character and our teaching or without maturing in our life along with our doctrine (1 Timothy 4:16).

This book addresses issues that we must consider in order to live as emotionally, spiritually, and relationally mature adults. This is not a "quick read" book as it contains scriptures to contemplate, personal sharing, paradigm-changing insights, and reflection questions. Prayer, journaling, and even discussing it with others are highly recommended. Chapter 1 defines what it means to love God with emotional intelligence and maturity. Not only are we born again spiritually, but in becoming emotionally healthy, we can also allow God to change our hearts and souls so that we can be "born again" emotionally and have the relationship with God and the life to the full that he has planned for us.

In Chapter 2 is the story of my personal battles and how I finally started to work through them at the heart and soul level. My emotional health and healing journey included dealing with perfectionism, depression, low self-esteem, and distorted beliefs. Once I began to process my emotional sewage, I was better able to accept, in my heart and soul, the things I had previously only been able to accept intellectually. I was able to break through spiritual and emotional strongholds and become a more healthy and whole person.

Chapter 3 reminds us that with God and his fellowship, we are never alone. It's reassuring to know that God promises that he is always with us no matter our state. Though Paul, in a healthy way, saw himself as the "worst of sinners," many of us have an unhealthy, toxic, shameful view of ourselves. We will also look at the progress and successes of the 12–step-type groups that met to discuss David Seamands' workbook entitled *Healing for Damaged Emotions*. God's grace, Satan's deadliest psychological weapon, perfectionism, and depression are also examined.

Testimonies of breakthroughs regarding disciples working on the sanctification necessary after baptism begin in Chapter 4.

Chapter 5 takes us on a journey that shows us how to build a strong biblical and spiritual foundation by discussing the authority of the Bible, discipleship, repentance, sin, and the forgiveness of sin. In this chapter I share parts of my own spiritual journey.

Chapter 6 encourages us to dig deeper in order to understand our true and whole self—spiritual, emotional, and mental. Pertinent concepts from Scriptures are provided that show how important spiritual and emotional wisdom and knowledge are in living out God's word.

Chapter 7 discusses the concept that insanity is doing the same thing over and over and expecting different results, in this case, attempting to address emotional issues with spiritual regimens alone even when this approach has previously failed to deliver us from character strongholds. I will share the repetitive behaviors and anesthetics that kept me in the cycle of "insanity" until professional counseling served as a vehicle for developing healthier paradigms and behaviors.

Chapter 8 discusses the enormous impact of our fathers on our lives. A dysfunctional father can be just as harmful as a father who is absent. In order for us to mature, we have to understand the impact of fathers (and our family of origin) on our view of God and on our spiritual and emotional well-being. The chapter ends with an encouraging discussion about God our perfect Father.

Chapter 9 focuses on the all-important change process. God has planned that all of his children be sanctified—that we become the "new creation" he has planned for us. Just as there are processes that are followed in order to recover from any type of physical injury or weakness, there are processes for character change and increasing emotional health. In John 15:11 (MSG), Jesus states, "I've told you these things for a purpose: that my joy might be your joy, and your joy wholly mature." I hope you'll join me and my personal heroes, five of whose testimonies are included, on the journey to live on God's solid food (Hebrews 5:11–14), experiencing his life to the full! We can do so only as we grow in our heart and soul love for God, ourselves, and each other.

> God is love. When we take up permanent residence in a life of love, we live in God and God lives in us. This way, love has the run of the house, becomes at home and *mature* in us, so that we're free of worry on Judgment Day—our standing in the world is identical with Christ's. There is no room in love for fear. Well-formed love banishes fear. Since fear is crippling, a fearful life—fear of death, fear of judgment—is one not yet fully formed in love (1 John 4:17–18 MSG, emphasis added).

Chapter One

What You Don't Know Will Hurt You

No man is free who is not master of himself. —*Epictetus*

The ancestor to every action is a thought.

—*Ralph Waldo Emerson*

One of my dear housemates, Jackie, had pains on one side of her body. She went to her doctor, who told her that she might have pulled a muscle and prescribed pain medicine. When the pain did not improve, Jackie returned to the doctor three times, and still the only diagnosis offered was a pulled muscle. Jackie discontinued the pain medication explaining to the doctors that it was ineffective, and on her next visit, she took a stronger stand and told the doctors that they needed to figure out what was going on. Months had passed with the doctors insisting that she had only a pulled muscle. The pain had not subsided and Jackie had no way of determining what the source of it could be without the help of her doctors. Finally, after Jackie persisted in pleading with the doctors to help her discover the problem, they ordered a colonoscopy. Though Jackie was past fifty, the age when everyone should have a colonoscopy, she had never had the procedure. Sure enough, the results showed irregularities leading the doctors to order additional tests. Jackie had an endoscopy and was admitted to the hospital. The tests revealed that she had Stage 4 colon cancer. Though Jackie looked great on the outside and remained very encouraging, Stage 4 colon cancer was destroying her body.

Just as Jackie and those around her were oblivious to what was going on inside of her, some of us live our lives perilously oblivious to the awful emotional dangers that are really going on inside us. A lack of awareness when it comes to our God-given emotions can lead to a lack of self-control, troubled relationships, unhealthy thinking, depression, anxiety, repetitive sin, and even suicidal thoughts. Unresolved issues that have not been effectively processed can wreak internal, external, and eternal havoc in our lives. A focus on changing behavior without addressing our heart and soul is dangerous. Jesus dealt with this type of situation with great alarm:

> "Woe to you, teachers of the law and Pharisees, you hypocrites! You clean the outside of the cup and dish, but inside they are full of greed and self-indulgence. Blind Pharisee! First clean the inside of the cup and dish, and then the outside also will be clean.
>
> "Woe to you, teachers of the law and Pharisees, you hypocrites! You are like whitewashed tombs, which look beautiful on the outside, but on the inside are full of the bones of the dead and everything unclean. In the same way, on the outside you appear to people as righteous but on the inside you are full of hypocrisy and wickedness" (Matthew 23:25–28).

Certainly, none of us want to live as tombs! Not even whitewashed tombs. No! We must understand what is happening inside.

Let's look at *The Message* version of this same passage for more insight:

> "You're hopeless, you religion scholars and Pharisees! Frauds! You burnish the surface of your cups and bowls so they sparkle in the sun, while the insides are maggoty with your greed and gluttony. Stupid Pharisee! Scour the insides, and then the gleaming surface will mean something.
>
> "You're hopeless, you religion scholars and Pharisees! Frauds! You're like manicured grave plots, grass clipped and the flowers bright, but six feet down its all rotting bones and worm-eaten flesh. People look at you and think you're saints, but beneath the skin you're total frauds."

Yes, Jesus painted a vivid picture and implored the people of his time to work on their insides. **Many of us have the desire to be godly but do not have sufficient tools to understand and change the inner core of our being.** We don't know how to become more like Jesus instead of just focusing on doing more things like Jesus.

Matthew Henry's Concise Commentary on the Bible discusses the "Crimes of the Pharisees" stating that

> The scribes and Pharisees were enemies to the gospel of Christ, and therefore to the salvation of the souls of men.... While they would seem to be godly, they were neither sober nor righteous. Outward motives may keep the outside clean, while the inside is filthy; but if the heart and spirit be made new, there will be newness of life; here we must begin with ourselves. The righteousness of the scribes and Pharisees was like the ornaments of a grave, or dressing up a dead body, only for show.[1]

Nowadays, some of us put a lot of effort into striving to act godly, forgetting that no matter how we may appear outwardly, we are what we are inwardly. Our goal is to be godly from the inside out.

REFLECTION:

How successful have you been with working on change from the inside out? Are you more likely to "gut it out" with surface changes or to "figure it out," uncovering the reason for behaviors, habits, and character weaknesses?

Unfortunately, we can forget that we are what we are inwardly. What would a test for emotional intelligence reveal? Would we score well beneath our comparable physical age? Are you chronologically an adult but still an emotional adolescent? We may find that our diagnosis would be Stage 4 Emotional Cancer! We may have the most beautiful looking cemetery plots, but inside they are plagued with maggots, rotten bones, and worm-eaten flesh. Sadly, too many disciples who really love God with all of their mind and strength are totally frustrated with something that they just can't seem to put their hand on or wrap their mind around.

We must also keep in mind that there is a stark difference between facing our personal sins and processing the impact of others' sins. Managing grief, loss, abuse, and hurts from others are God-given processes that should not be confused with repentance from sin. The process of grief or loss (sometimes even triggered by positive events) typically can include shock, numbness, anger, denial, pain, guilt, bargaining, isolation, depression, reflection, loneliness, reconstruction, acceptance, and hope. We can quickly disciple people's attitudes about and reactions to being sinned against without realizing that we all need time to work through such occurrences. We can shame people's feelings about being harmed and not allow them to do what humans do: react to harm so they can process it. Just last night, a wonderful friend called himself ungrateful. Such self-incrimination was faulty. The reality is that due to greedy corporate franchisers, he just lost his business. He's reorienting his career, understanding his new life as a disciple, and dealing with a very challenging mother of his child.

My heart still breaks when I think of a family member who was physically abused by her husband multiple times a week. As a result of ignorance and arrogance, her spiritual mentors told her that she needed to figure out what she must change so that her husband would not beat her! Honestly, I felt like giving them and her husband a beating. We must know the difference between personal sin and the God-given processes for dealing with grief or loss and others' sins against us so that we will not heap additional and faulty emotional maltreatment on ourselves and other people.

Furthermore, we must not forget how prevalent mental illness is in our society (see Appendix I). It's been swept under the rug for a long time. We forget that many of us grew up in emotionally unhealthy or dysfunctional situations. We may not have acquired healthy coping, problem solving, and relationship skills. Many Christians are still carrying this heavy baggage. In *Hurt People Hurt People*, Sandra Wilson, PhD states, "When people try to function in areas that affect their untended wounds and unhealed hurts, they inevitably hurt others. **Often they wound others as severely as they were hurt, and in remarkably similar ways.**"[2]

The following statistics highlight a few of the ways that people experience hurt and pain in different life situations:

- An estimated 26.2 percent of Americans ages 18 and older—about one in four adults—suffer from a diagnosable mental disorder in a given year.[3] That's 57.7 million people!

- There are between 960,000 and 3 million incidents of violence against a current or former spouse, boyfriend, or girlfriend per year.[4]

- More than one fifth (23.3 percent) of people 12 or older (that's about 58.1 million people!) participated in binge drinking at least once in the last 30 days.[5]

- Over 3 million reports of child abuse are made every year in the United States. In 2007, approximately 5.8 million children were involved in an estimated 3.2 million child abuse reports and allegations.[6]

REFLECTION:

Have you noticed any ways that you have hurt yourself or others in the same way you have been hurt?

_____

_____

_____

Heart and Soul

As disciples, we want to love God with ALL of our being. But what exactly is our heart and what is our soul? What we don't know or understand about these crucial elements of our being can hurt our relationship with God, ourselves, and others. So let's take a closer look.

Various dictionaries define the soul as "the principle of life, feeling, thought, and action in humans; the spiritual part of humans as distinct from the physical part; the emotional part of human nature; the seat of the feelings or sentiment; the animating principle; the essential element or part of something; the inspirer or moving spirit of some action, movement, etc."

Various dictionaries define the heart as "the center of the total personality, especially with reference to intuition, feeling, or emotion; the center of emotion, especially as contrasted to the head as the center of the intellect; the capacity for sympathy; feeling; affection; spirit, courage, or enthusiasm."

Did you catch those definitions? *Please* read them again. God didn't just make us physical beings. God didn't just make us beings with intellect. God doesn't just want our mind and strength. God is unbelievably amazing. He gives us *all* of himself. He made us to live in a love relationship with him with *all* of ourselves. **God wants our emotions, our sentiments, our affection, our enthusiasm, the vital center of our being.** He wants our deepest and sincerest feelings, and our deepest and sincerest beliefs. He wants what constitutes our being, the seat or headquarters of our thoughts and even imagination. That is what God wants from us, and isn't that what we also want in our closest relationships?

What blows me away is God's loving rationale for his greatest commandment in Mark 12:30: "Love the Lord your God with all your heart and with all your soul and with all your mind and with all your strength." In Deuteronomy 6:1–3, Moses told God's people:

> "This is the commandment, the rules and regulations, that God, your God, commanded me to teach you to live out in the land you're about to cross into to possess. *This is so that* you'll live in deep reverence before God lifelong, observing all his rules and regulations that I'm commanding you, you and your children and your grandchildren, living good long lives.
>
> Listen obediently, Israel. Do what you're told *so that you'll have a good life, a life of abundance and bounty*, just as God promised, in a land abounding in milk and honey" (MSG, emphasis added).

God wants this not for him, but for us!

Though disciples have given their all to God, I have encountered many who have felt "blocked" or "stuck" in their spiritual or personal growth—despite efforts to increase Bible study, prayer, fasting, and Christian service. My prayer is that this book will catapult you past these blocks and along your journey to live with greater joy and a deeper reverence for God. There is no need for any of us to be stuck, clogged, or burdened. Continuously working on our mind and strength love for God (through more study and greater obedience) without addressing our insides will only cause greater frustration and possibly even throwing in the towel spiritually. **We cannot have the relationship with God that he has planned for us (John 10:10) without being healthy emotionally.** Thank God that there is a way that we can be free—unstuck, unclogged, unburdened—to love God with all our heart and soul.

REFLECTION:

How do you feel about God's rationale for his greatest commandment? What does God's rationale reveal about his character and love?

_____

_____

_____

The Greatest Commandment

In Matthew 22:36–37 Jesus was asked, "Teacher, which is the greatest commandment in the Law?" He replied, "'Love the Lord your God with all your heart and with all your soul and with all your mind.' This is the first and greatest commandment." To command means to direct with specific authority; or to issue an order. In our worldwide fellowship (see www.disciplestoday.com), few would ever question the disciples' obedience in their efforts to love God with all of our mind and strength. Our fellowship has prided itself in its commitment to living as disciples of Christ with the Bible as our standard.

But loving God with all of our mind and strength is just part of God's command. In the "greatest commandment," Jesus also addressed the emotional and mental aspects of our being. We must grow and mature to the point of being free enough to love God with all of our heart and soul.

Mind and strength issues are usually much easier to see, address, and measure. Heart and soul, love and concern, on the other hand, are usually a bit more challenging. Yet, we all know that we can't pick and choose the portion of Scripture with which we feel more comfortable (see 2 Timothy 3:16). Nor can we ignore the challenging areas that we feel ill-equipped to address. In order to more fully obey God, we need to grow in our ability to love God wholly—with all of our being, with our heart and soul, not just our mind and strength.

Moreover, professional plumbers tell us that most drain clogs are caused by the gradual accumulation of organic matter, hair, and grease on the inside walls of drainpipes. If the gunk is not cleaned out, it will build up over time and slow down the normal flow of water through the pipes. The same can be said of our hearts and souls. Some of us have "clogs" that prevent us from experiencing the joys of an uninhibited love relationship with God and others. Deuteronomy 6:5–9 in The Message version says,

> Love GOD, your God, with your whole heart: love him with all that's in you, love him with all you've got!
>
> Write these commandments that I've given you today on your hearts. Get them inside of you and then get them inside your children. Talk about them wherever you are, sitting at home or walking in the street; talk about them from the time you get up in the morning to when you fall into bed at night. Tie them on your hands and foreheads as a reminder; inscribe them on the doorposts of your homes and on your city gates.

It is obvious that God wants all of us—not just our mind and our strength. He wants us to get his commandments inside of us. As a result of circumstances in my youth, I was emotionally "clogged up" to the point where I could not accept (beyond intellectual acknowledgment) God's love and therefore could not love him in return with all of my heart and soul. At the same time, I doubt that anyone would have ever questioned my mind and strength love for Jehovah God. I was once told by a friend that it made them tired just looking at me and all of my activities. I was continually focused on my relationship with God and was tirelessly about his business. But despite all my hypervigilant efforts, I didn't know and couldn't understand how to truly love with my heart and soul.

REFLECTION:

Do you feel in touch with the heart and soul parts of you? How import-
ant do you feel these God-given parts are? What types of "clogs" exist in
your heart, soul, and relationships?

_____

_____

_____

Expectations

In the introduction to Job in The Message Remix version of the Bible, the author, Eugene Peterson, says that there is more to the book of Job than Job himself—there are Job's friends. I highly recommend that you take time to read the entire introduction, where Peterson explains:

> The moment we find ourselves in trouble of any kind—sick in the hospital, bereaved by a friend's death, dismissed from a job or relationship, depressed or bewildered—people start showing up telling us exactly what is wrong with us and what we must do to get better. Sufferers attract fixers the way roadkills attract vultures. At first we are impressed that they bother with us and amazed at their facility with answers. They know so much! How did they get to be such experts at living?
>
> More often than not, these people use the Word of God frequently and loosely. They are full of spiritual diagnosis and prescription. It all sounds so hopeful. But then we begin to wonder, "Why is it that, for all their apparent compassion, we feel worse instead of better after they've said their piece?" After Job listens to his three religious friends offer their re-ligious opinions, he painfully and emphatically protests. As God subsequently speaks, Job becomes silent with awestruck faith.[7]

Peterson's take on Job is profoundly insightful, illuminating, and in-structive. He further notes that "real faith cannot be reduced to spiritual bromides and merchandised in success stories. It is refined in the lives and the storms of pain." Peterson continues to share that we cannot separate the truth about God from the heart of God.

Naturally, few people like to see others suffer. We may try to prevent, deny, ignore, or alleviate suffering. But, with the heart of Jesus, we have to pray to not be like Job's friends, who presumed that they could fix or improve things. We may indeed see our suffering friends and imagine how they could have improved relationships, families, and balance in their personal, spiritual, emotional, mental, professional, physical, or financial lives. But as we look to be better friends and help carry each other's burdens, let's make sure we see the transformative beauty and holiness that can be gained in suffering.

I hope and pray that as you read this book, my mistakes, education, personal and professional experiences, volunteer efforts, and personal growth can lead you and your loved ones to more freedom, depth, and joy in your heart and soul relationship with God. I am not a believer in quick fixes or simplistic solutions from "experts." I emphatically believe that **we will not attain to God's plan for our spiritual lives without thoroughly addressing his plan for our emotional (heart and soul) world.** I have seen the ill effects—sometimes spiritually lethal effects—of spiritual misdiagnoses and prescriptions. Constantly spiritualizing emotional issues has hurt many disciples. It is harmful to place labels of selfishness and pride, absent of informed, emotionally intelligent specifics which address core emotional issues. Shallow (mind and strength only), secular wisdom oftentimes pushes us further away from God.

Throughout this book we will not only address the kind of suffering Job experienced—Satan's temptations—but also how to handle more effectively the type of suffering that is a result of a lack of emotional intelligence or maturity. Just as we are called to be born again spiritually, we need to also ensure that we are "born again" in our heart and soul, emotionally and psychologically. Though we receive the Holy Spirit when we are baptized, we are called to add to our faith in order to become more like Jesus and to make our calling and election sure (2 Peter 1). This is a process that requires daily decisions, commitment, and great courage. Though God, through Christ's sacrifice, sees us as sin-free, once we are baptized, we must continuously address our character issues. Many lives can drastically improve—the effectiveness and productivity talked about in 2 Peter 1—with an effort to address the emotional aspects of our God-given being, as they are a major component in forming our character.

In the pages to come, we will discuss the suffering and self-sabotage that can be diminished with greater emotional intelligence, health, and healing. We will also provide information that can lead to a greater emotional aptitude and more freedom as we face the challenges of our lives. Our goal is not that we only survive and barely make it into heaven, but that we have faith that is refined in the storms of pain. We can experience the miracles Eugene Peterson describes: "When these people go through suffering, their lives are often transformed, deepened, marked with beauty and holiness, in remarkable ways that could never have been anticipated before the suffering."[8] Such miracles can happen when we go after a heart and soul love for God. We can benefit from a greater degree of healing and thus a greater degree of freedom in our love relationship with him.

REFLECTION:

What new convictions have you gained from this chapter? How do you want to enhance your relationship with God? What decision(s) would be helpful in your efforts to be transformed into the likeness of Jesus Christ (Romans 8:29)?

_____

_____

_____

Chapter Two

My Emotional Health and Healing Journey

For many reasons, I should not have been able to accomplish all that God has blessed me to do. Children of poverty, divorce, and generational dysfunctions statistically have so much stacked against them. Despite having few positive role models, I achieved career success and was very fruitful spiritually. Yet I did not work on my emotional health until I started reading intently about personal growth and then started professional counseling on a consistent basis in 2003. Since then, I have been able to work through many challenges, grieve losses and traumas that I had attempted to ignore, and reframe events for which I incorrectly took responsibility. Even with all this growth, I, like all of us, am still a work in progress.

In many ways, God has blessed me beyond all I could ask or imagine (Ephesians 3:20). I've had amazing opportunities despite our family struggling financially once my parents separated. From the time I was in third grade, I knew I wanted to be a teacher and impact students just like my favorite teacher, Mr. Fiandra, did. As a result of the turmoil and dysfunction in my childhood environment, I did what I could to figure out how to get the love and approval that every child needs. By working really hard, I sought after inner peace, making an impact, having a decent future, and winning approval. I not only trained as a teacher but also obtained master's degrees in both education and business administration. I started my career teaching math, and a number of years later, I worked for the state Department of Education in New Jersey and then as a vice principal and principal. Subsequently, I was able to work in school district central administration offices as a math and/or science supervisor. Though many in my immediate and extended family really struggled, I vigilantly focused on beating the odds and "making it." Another marvelous blessing was the opportunity to serve as an officer of the Association of Mathematics Teachers of New Jersey for five years and then as only the third African

-American president of that organization in 100 years.

I was just as driven in my spiritual life. After being baptized, I don't remember ever not being a "leader." I was serious about my relationship with God, grateful that I was understanding the Bible, grateful that I had people of whom I could ask spiritual questions, very grateful for my salvation, and sharing the gospel with as many people as possible. After completing graduate school at the University of Georgia, I was able to do a summer internship in our Atlanta church and then continue working as a math teacher. Not only was I frequently in Bible studies, but, as a small group leader, I was given responsibility to mentor other small group leaders. Ironically, even though I was much younger and single, I was even asked to mentor older and married women. If anyone needed anything, I prided myself in being a "go to" person who was reliable and who could get the job done!

Yet, despite great blessings and numerous successes, there was an internal battle that never seemed to stop. I had not really paid much attention to my inner self. I was "successful" spiritually, academically, and in my career. Even as a disciple, I was intently focused on achieving results and had no idea how to deal with emotional health and healing issues.

Never Enough

It turned out that perfectionism was choking the life out of me. Funny thing is, I actually thought that perfectionism was a good thing. In fact, throughout business school, since one strategy was to share a weakness that can also be viewed as a strength, I learned to use perfectionism as a "weakness" during interviews because employers would appreciate that quality. In other words, though perfectionism is a debilitating and imprisoning way of living, employers would appreciate someone who paid attention to details and wanted to do the job right. The problem was that my need to have things be "just right" was full of unhealthy hyper-vigilance. My "do," "don't do," "could have," "should have," and "if only" thoughts took up way too much space in my head each day and during many nights of sleepless anxiety.

I finally decided that my emotional health needed to be a priority. I had prayed and prayed and prayed, fasted, sought advice, served, worked, planned, and begged God to help me grow. But it wasn't until I went to counseling that I was able to take steps to better ensure that I would not repeat the dysfunctional cycles of past generations.

Overcoming the perfectionism that permeated every part of my life was a laborious process. Being able to clear out my emotional sewage and thus have room in my heart and soul for God's grace and undeserved kindness helped me to lessen my compulsive need to be "perfect." I had to psychologically reframe and grieve the traumatic situations and losses in my life. The way I had tried to put the past behind me and move on just wasn't working. Unprocessed grief stays with us. **Healing is not a simple, linear, or easy process;** "it involves growing in grace, reprogramming our minds, and healing in every level of our lives."[1] I am so grateful to God for this scripture in Isaiah:

> *Surely he took up our pain*
> *and bore our suffering,*
> yet we considered him punished by God,
> stricken by him, and afflicted.
> But he was pierced for our transgressions,
> he was crushed for our iniquities;
> the punishment that brought us peace was on him,
> and *by his wounds we are healed.*
> We all, like sheep, have gone astray,
> each of us has turned to our own way;
> and the LORD has laid on him
> the iniquity of us all.
>
> Therefore I will give him a portion among the great,
> and he will divide the spoils with the strong,
> because he poured out his life unto death,
> and was numbered with the transgressors.
> For he bore the sin of many,
> and made intercession for the transgressors
> (Isaiah 53:4–6, 12, emphasis added).

Since my mom and dad and others around me seemed to focus on completing tasks and were very successful at it, I believed that I needed to endlessly strive to do the same and that God also was all about the results. But that is not the heart of God. It's hard to change this mindset that I developed over two decades. Since I now know that **changing any habit or way of living is a process** that is just beginning when we decide to repent, in order to be free we all must surrender to the process of emotional healing. I hope that we can stop fighting God and ignoring our emotions and join him in this process of transforming our hearts and souls. (Additional and more specific information on the change process is included in Chapter 9 and Appendix III.)

David Seamands, author of the *Healing for Damaged Emotions Workbook,* discusses five areas of emotional healing that have been fundamental for me:

1. The mind—distorted concepts
2. The feelings—damaged emotions
3. Perceptions—downgrading evaluations
4. Relationships—disruptive contradictions
5. Memories—past hurts that replay in the present and interfere with the way you live.[2]

My struggle with perfectionism resulted from all of these emotional infirmities. I had learned not to trust myself and had many distorted concepts. I didn't trust my feelings; since they were seldom validated, I suppressed them instead. But they did not disappear. Suppressed grief and sadness turned into depression and anxiety. I negatively evaluated many situations and lived waiting for the next shoe to drop. Since I took on the responsibility of making sure that my emotionally unavailable father and alcoholic stepfather were not annoyed, I learned to take too much responsibility for others' unhealthy behaviors. This is the essence of codependency. In some professional settings, since I had not successfully resolved past hurts, these subconscious issues showed up as triggers in work relationships. Of course they also showed up in some of my relationships in the fellowship of the church.

Since I grew up trying to stay out of trouble, with being a "good girl" and a people-pleaser as my modus operandi for gaining love and acceptance, the real me—my inner child, the composite of my feelings, natural talents, and the unique dimensions of my personality—didn't have a safe, warm, and nurturing childhood. The real me needed to be loved. I frequently felt shame; I felt that I was unlovable, not good enough. On the other hand, the perfectionist me was accustomed to denying legitimate emotions that needed fair and proper expression. I had learned that anger and conflict were bad; they meant trouble. I avoided trouble as much as possible. I was beyond tired of hearing constant fussing at home. In uncovering the real me, I had to deal with the fact that I never thought about whether or not I was happy. When Chris Reed (former Philadelphia evangelist) once asked me if I was happy, I had to ask for a definition! I robbed myself of spiritual and emotional growth and a friendship with God by trying to keep the real, heart-and-soul me hidden.

Through counseling and discussion groups, I came to further accept the good, bad, and ugly about myself and my strengths and weaknesses, just as God does. God really does want to heal you and change you in order that the "real you" can become the person he created you to be. 2 Corinthians 10:12–13, 17–18 encourages us:

> We do not dare to classify or compare ourselves with some who commend themselves. When they measure themselves by themselves and compare themselves with themselves, they are not wise. We, however, will not boast beyond proper limits, but will confine our boasting to the sphere of service God himself has assigned to us, a sphere that also includes you… But, "Let the one who boasts boast in the Lord." For it is not the one who commends himself who is approved, but the one whom the Lord commends.

Unquestionably, as Psalm 51:6 tells us, **God desires truth in the inner parts.** He wants to teach us wisdom in the innermost place. He wants to deal with the real me and the real you!

REFLECTION:

Would you consider yourself to be a perfectionist in any areas of your life? Has that modus operandi worked for you? Have you been able to accept and love the good, the bad, and all the "ugly" parts of you as God has?

Dealing with Depression

After seeing my counselor for a while, she mentioned that she believed that I had been depressed for about twenty years. As busy as I was in the church and at work, I would have described myself as a Type-AAA, not just a Type-A Personality. Nobody would have ever thought that I was depressed. It took me quite a while to accept that I was, and even longer to accept that I needed to take medication for anxiety and depression. I would feel most depressed when I thought of my family or my financial debt and when I felt that I was all alone with no one protecting me, providing for me, or caring. It was even harder when I realized that many seemed to think that I could take care of myself and them too. Since I had such a challenging relationship with my father, I usually felt depressed after seeing him. I would actually go shopping almost every time I saw him. I later learned that I was probably subconsciously thinking that I would take care of myself by shopping since I didn't feel that he took care of me.

As a disciple, when I felt bad, I would share my thoughts, but no one ever suggested that I might be depressed. I also actually felt that I shouldn't feel sad or depressed since I am a Christian. Satan wins when we allow him to turn our temporary or prolonged feelings of depression into spiritual defeat, doubt, and despondence. In order to properly deal with these types of challenges, though it's all connected, we need to be able to differentiate the emotional from the spiritual. My personal strategies for overcoming depression have been psychiatrist-prescribed medication, exercise, and, through professional counseling, dealing with the core issues that led to depression. Reading, praying, fasting, and working harder for God didn't fix my anxiety and depression. Christian disciplines alone will not fix chemical mental health issues.

Regrettably, I typically ignored my physical, emotional, and spiritual limitations. I did not take care of myself as God would have me do. I didn't make myself a priority and certainly had no idea that living with others' shortcomings and the injustices of my past could lead to depression. Since traumatic events were identified and discussed during my Bible studies but were not effectively dealt with on an emotional level, I did not heal those emotions. As a result, I have had complications in some relationships. It was especially hard to trust others since I grew up feeling that I could not trust my caretakers to protect me and make me a priority. Acknowledging and learning about depression or any other emotional challenge is the beginning of taking positive steps toward healing. If we are courageous enough to tackle such issues, we can say with Paul:

> But we have this treasure in jars of clay to show that *this all-surpassing power is from God and not from us.* We are hard pressed on every side, but not crushed; perplexed, but not in despair; persecuted, but not abandoned; struck down, but not destroyed... Therefore we do not lose heart. Though outwardly we are wasting away, yet inwardly we are being *renewed day by day* (2 Corinthians 4:7–9, 16, emphasis added).

Learning to Take Care of Myself

How we see and feel about ourselves deeply affects our relationships with God, ourselves, and others. Christian psychologists note that there are three components of a healthy self-image: a sense of belongingness, of worthwhileness, and of competence. Countless folks feel that they just don't belong. Subconsciously, as children, we all internalized others' opinions of ourselves. For most of us, our parents had the most influence on how we see ourselves today. The reflections of the relationships with the most significant adults in our lives are the foundation of our esteem. As children, we didn't have the ability to filter out the unhealthy opinions of others.

Personally, my distorted self-image had adversely affected my relationships with God and with other people in that I always felt that I had to earn acceptance and love. I couldn't fully accept people's love or God's freely given love. This all goes back to the root of me not feeling nurtured or important as a child. Though my parents did the best they could, soft skills were not in surplus and their own emotional bank accounts were in the red; they had little to give in these crucial areas. Thus, I typically felt less than valued or competent and needed the constant approval of others. These feelings made it very hard to accept, in my heart, that I am a beloved child of God.

Fortunately, once we are able to effectively deal with the historical events that have led to our low self-esteem, we can be free to accept God's view of us with all of our heart and soul:

> See what great love the Father has lavished on us, that we
> should be called *children of God!* And that is what we are! The
> reason the world does not know us is that it did not know
> him. Dear friends, now we are children of God, and what we
> will be has not yet been made known. But we know that when
> Christ appears, we shall be like him, for we shall see him as
> he is (1 John 3:1–2, emphasis added).

Naturally, cleaning out the emotional sewage and subsequently being able to accept how God views me made all the difference in how I see myself. And it can do the same for you!

Though Jesus has commanded us to love our neighbors as we love ourselves (Matthew 22:39), too many of us do not believe that proper self-love is the "only sure foundation on which to build loving relationships with other people."[3] For many years, I believed that I should not think of my own needs at all, but only the needs of others. These thoughts started when I was a child with separated parents and in the home of an alcoholic. My stepfather was the one we all tried to keep happy. The same situation existed when I was with my biological father. It seemed to always be about him. Then, as a disciple, I had heard that J-O-Y came from putting "Jesus first, Others second, and Yourself last." Self-love and self-interest did not seem like godly things.

I continuously left out one important word in a scripture I'd thought I understood: "Each of you should look not only to your own interests, but also to the interests of others." In context, Philippians 2 says, "Do nothing out of selfish ambition or vain conceit, but in humility consider others better than yourselves. Each of you should look not only to your own interests, but also to the interests of others." Since I didn't feel that I was a priority to the adults in my life, I transferred those thoughts and feelings into my Christian life. Between this take on Philippians 2 and all the scriptures about denying ourselves, I didn't think that I was supposed to make my needs a priority. I did not properly take care of myself and thus I found myself at times feeling bitter when I gave to others. Since my emotional bank account usually had a negative balance, I really had little of value I could give to others from a healthy position.

Without changing the way I saw myself and despite the fact that God used many people to show me how much he loves, affirms, and accepts me, it seemed impossible for me to love and accept myself. In order for us to do as God commands: "Love the Lord your God with all your heart and with all your soul and with all your mind...and...*Love your neighbor as yourself*" (Matthew 22:37–39, emphasis added), we really have to allow him to heal our low self-esteem. With a healthy self-esteem, we will be able to love from a more pure heart the way God intended.

REFLECTION:

How important is it for you to love and take care of yourself? How do overburdened people make others feel? How did Jesus take care of himself?

Chapter Three

You Are Not Alone:
The Power
of Healing Discussion Groups

You probably know Michael Jackson's great song, "You Are Not Alone." He sings about love and isolation in desperate and anguished times. The songwriter (R. Kelly) says in the song that his friend is in his heart and that he will be there for them. Most of us wish for a dream relationship with someone who will always be there for us. Many of us would love to be rescued every once in a while from the troubles and hardships of our lives. Personally, I'm ready for heaven and with John I will say, "Amen. Come, Lord Jesus" (Revelation 22:20). Once we're in heaven, we will be with God forever. But we don't need to wait for healthy relationship connections until then!

The good news is that as disciples we are commanded to love, bear with, forgive, encourage, agree with, build up, honor, accept, instruct, greet, submit to, be devoted to, confess our sins to, teach, admonish, and pray for each other. God also calls us to live in harmony with each other. He instructs us to be kind and compassionate, to have equal concern for, to be at peace with, and offer hospitality to each other. There are numerous scriptures that discuss how we should relate to one another. God wants us to spur one another on and tell the truth to each other. As the body of Christ, we are all connected to each other. With God's fellowship, we are never alone. The even greater blessing is that Scripture promises us that our God himself is always with us in the now:

> No temptation has overtaken you except what is common to mankind. And God is faithful; he will not let you be tempted beyond what you can bear. But when you are tempted, he will also provide a way out so that you can endure it (1 Corinthians 10:13).

"And surely I am with you always, to the very end of the age" (Matthew 28:20).

"As I was with Moses, so I will be with you; I will never leave you nor forsake you" (Joshua 1:5).

"How much more will your Father in heaven give the Holy Spirit to those who ask him!" (Luke 11:13).

"But the Advocate, the Holy Spirit, whom the Father will send in my name, will teach you all things and will remind you of everything I have said to you" (John 14:26).

Peter replied, "Repent and be baptized, every one of you, in the name of Jesus Christ for the forgiveness of your sins. And you will receive the gift of the Holy Spirit" (Acts 2:38).

Unfortunately, some disciples know these scriptures but express that they haven't felt them in their heart and soul. Though we have the head knowledge that there really is nothing new under the sun (Ecclesiastes 1:9), **we are frequently tempted to believe that our struggles, sins, emotional battles, insecurities, infirmities, anger, wounds, fears, and thoughts are vastly different from everyone else's.** A number of disciples, in an unhealthy way, believe that their sins are far worse than anyone else's. But God assures us that they are not and that he is with us. He will carry us through.

REFLECTION:

Which scriptures resonate most with you? Why? Do the "one another" scriptures describe your personal relationships in your fellowship?

_____

_____

_____

You have probably heard many sermons, pep talks, motivational speakers, and teachers. Constructivist educators and social researchers have attempted to impress upon teachers and speakers the fact that the least effective way of helping others is through speaking alone. Information is least retained through such means. While personal transformation can begin with listening to a speaker or reading a book, it rarely comes to fruition without reflection, processing, and discussing areas of desired growth. A safe place is needed for emotional growth to occur.

Next to God's word, David Seamands' *Healing for Damaged Emotions Workbook[1]* is my all-time favorite book. When used together with the power of God's word, the workbook discussion questions provide a framework for the most powerful type of capacity-building and life-changing sharing I have ever witnessed. Using this tool, groups of courageous disciples and friends have met over the past few years to discuss ways to grow in our hearts and souls and to more effectively deal with situations that have impacted our lives. I highly recommend that single-gender discipleship groups, community groups, and other kinds of groups work through Seamands' book with twelve-step-like guidelines for group sharing. Unlike typical discipleship groups led by one person, this type of group operates as a safe place for people to think through, discuss, uncover, and focus on their own lives, struggles, sins, shortcomings, and infirmities. Twelve-step-format guidelines for starting a discussion group are available on my website (www.cresendajones.com).

Psychotherapy (professional counseling) and the group of women I regularly met with in this type of setting helped me tremendously in my journey of emotional healing and growth. **Past issues that have not been effectively processed cannot be left behind.** Christian psychologists note that despite the age-old adage, time does *not* heal all wounds. Though I discussed everything I could think of in 1985 as I went through a Bible-study series on how to become a disciple of Jesus, I came to understand that **there is a major difference between talking about situations and emotionally resolving them on a heart level.** In order to recall and process my most impactful life events and emotions, I desperately needed the women in the group to hear my stories and I needed to hear their stories. The group helped me to feel that I am not alone in my pain or my emotional health goals. My hope is that as we share our stories in this book, you will find comfort in knowing that you are not alone in your thoughts, feelings, pain, and efforts toward recovery and personal growth.

Family-of-Origin Issues

When a discussion group first begins, each participant shares their family-of-origin story. With every group, from the Bahamas to the Bronx, this sharing of stories immediately creates a close bond among the participants. Sharing your story is freeing. Since most of us do not grow up in functional families, many of our stories are heartrending. Yet, at the same time, as Acts 3:19 says, we can begin to experience times of refreshing as we begin to talk about things that we have never before effectively processed.

In discussion groups I have been a part of, I have heard a great deal about family-of-origin issues. These are defined as the range of emotional and relational issues that can be connected to a person's experiences with parents, primary caregivers, and families in general. Women I have known would share about their parents' separation, how scared they were when their parents would fight, and how their fathers were impossible to please. One sister shared how she left home when she was fifteen because it was a horrible place to be. Sadly, her father had abused her sexually. Personally, one of my biggest challenges growing up was that I didn't know how to deal with my stepfather's alcoholism. I did my best to be the "invisible child" while my sister and brother were the ones usually in trouble. I didn't want any of the negative attention that was doled out from my stepfather, so I did what I could to stay out of his way. I suppressed my emotions for a very long time. Sometimes, after stuffing my feelings for far too long, I would blurt out frustrations to my mom. I was not in touch with my feelings, so I certainly was not able to effectively express them or respond to them in a healthy way. I did not know how to heal from my past to be able to move forward.

REFLECTION:

Have you shared your life story and most significant events with your closest friends? Do you feel resolved about the most impactful events of your life? Do you know and feel resolved about your family-of-origin issues?

_____

_____

As the healing groups I have been a part of have progressed, participants have come to understand that **we are *not* automatically healed of past emotional damage when we become Christians.** We've discussed persistent problems, fears, past pain, and how we feel about God working in these areas. So many have shared that in spite of prayer, Bible study, fasting, and implementing advice, they still struggle with relationships, depression, anxiety, panic attacks, suicidal thoughts, and insecurity. Some feel that they can't go to professional counseling since they don't think they can handle the pain of bringing up everything that happened in their past. If we don't deal with these issues and unhealthy paradigms, they will likely wreak havoc in our lives. Many have shared that they have persistent problems with inferiority, perfectionism, hypersensitivity, fear, and sexuality. It's reassuring to know Romans 8:26–27:

> In the same way, the Spirit helps us in our weakness. We do not know what we ought to pray for, but the Spirit himself intercedes for us through wordless groans. And he who searches our *hearts* knows the mind of the Spirit, because the Spirit intercedes for God's people in accordance with the will of God (emphasis added).

REFLECTION:

Have you believed the familiar saying, "Time heals all wounds"? Why is that not true?

_____

_____

_____

Helping Each Other Embrace God's Forgiveness

Equally as important as family-of-origin issues, in my support groups we discuss the idea that **"only after you have accepted God's unconditional forgiveness are you set free to forgive others."**[2] Too many of us haven't been able to forgive ourselves, though we intellectually know that God has forgiven us. Despite the fact that some traumatic events are not our fault, we can carry guilt and shame, not be able to accept God's grace, and become debt collectors in our own lives and with others. Even when we have sinned, it can be a major struggle to let ourselves off the hook as God does. Too many of us automatically and subconsciously base our relationship with God on the "do and don't do" messages of the church or our families. People have shared about the pain they felt when those who abused them denied it or told them, "What happens in this house stays in the house." They have also shared their difficulties with forgiveness and trust.

I am amazed by the reactions of many families when a child tells them that they have been abused. Many times, families that don't know how to deal with abuse simply try to ignore it. These situations have severely damaged too many women, men, and families. I personally felt that my dad should have been there for me as I was dealing with the fallout from my parents' divorce and my stepfather's alcoholism. Unfortunately, he didn't know what to do. Since my parents were typically immersed in their own challenges, as a child I did all I knew how to do. I worked to perform, achieve, and strive for perfection. This became an endless treadmill of looking for acceptance, attention, and love, which carried on into my adult life and my relationship with God. Thank God that we can ask him to "forgive us our debts, as we also have forgiven our debtors" (Matthew 6:12).

The support groups also discussed the idea of Jesus being our "Wounded Healer," one of the chapter titles in the *Healing for Damaged Emotions Workbook*. Hebrews 4:14–16 says:

> Therefore, since we have a great high priest who has ascended into heaven, Jesus the Son of God, let us hold firmly to the faith we profess. For we do not have a high priest who is unable to empathize with our weaknesses, but we have one who has been tempted in every way, just as we are—yet he

did not sin. Let us then approach God's throne of grace with confidence, so that we may receive mercy and find grace to help us in our time of need.

Indeed, I am so grateful that Jesus is sensitive and fully compassionate regarding my pain! I don't feel all alone when I know that others have experienced similar situations, understand me, and care for me. My damaged emotions and character infirmities sabotaged my happiness and relationships. Seamands encourages us by saying that "because of what Jesus suffered emotionally in his humanity, you can be certain that God knows, cares, and fully understands your feelings of woundedness."[3] His understanding is comforting!

REFLECTION:

Have you forgiven yourself as God has forgiven you? Have you let yourself off the hook? What situation has been most difficult with regard to forgiving yourself?

Depression

The healing discussion groups read, answer questions, and discuss two chapters on depression. Unfortunately, it is believed that twelve percent of adults in the USA suffer from depression in any given year.[4] Women are at least twice as likely as men to experience episodes of severe depression. When someone is suffering from depression, it affects all aspects of their lives. There are emotional, motivational, behavioral, cognitive, spiritual, and physical symptoms. Most people who are depressed feel sad, dejected, miserable, empty, or humiliated. They usually feel anxious, angry, and agitated. Many experience crying spells and lose interest in their usual activities. They become less active and less productive. Many depressed people have negative views of self and shame about who they are. Pessimism, procrastination, and suicidal thoughts can occur. Physical ailments such as headaches, constipation, dizzy spells, general pain, fatigue, and disturbed appetite and sleep are also common with depression. David Seamands states that as a Christian we will experience feelings of depression, but should "not view it as spiritual failure, but simply as a normal part of life."[5]

Even the psalmist seemed to speak of feelings of depression in Psalm 42:5-7 and verse 3:

> Why, my soul, are you downcast?
>> Why so disturbed within me?
> Put your hope in God,
>> for I will yet praise him,
>> my Savior and my God.
> My soul is downcast within me;
>> therefore I will remember you
> from the land of the Jordan,
>> the heights of Hermon—from Mount Mizar.
> Deep calls to deep
>> in the roar of your waterfalls;
> all your waves and breakers
>> have swept over me.

> My tears have been my food
>> day and night,
> while people say to me all day long,
>> "Where is your God?"

Jeremiah is a man of God who may have suffered from depression. He was called the weeping prophet. The Bible clearly shows the intense emotions of many people. Though we readily accept the chemical imbalance that exists in diabetics, for example, we somehow mistake feelings of depression, which may be the result of a similar imbalance, as a spiritual issue rather than a medical one. My prayer is that we increase our knowledge so that people with medical, mental, and physical issues won't be incorrectly viewed as unspiritual.

REFLECTION:

What's been your understanding of depression? Who in the Bible processed feelings of depression? Can you recognize symptoms of depression? Why would it be harmful to label medical issues as spiritual deficits?

Satan's Deadliest Weapon

What would you say is Satan's deadliest weapon in our world today? From social advocates and a variety of pulpits I've heard all types of suggestions: immorality, materialism, being deceived, lack of knowledge of God's word, and apathy. Of course we have the letters to all of the churches in Revelation where Christian churches were challenged: Ephesus about their first love, Pergamum about allowing false teachings, Thyatira for tolerating Jezebel who called herself a prophetess and yet led people to immorality and adultery, Sardis for having a reputation of being alive but being dead with incomplete deeds, and Laodicea for being lukewarm.

Our groups discussed Satan's weapons of fear, doubt, anger, hostility, worry, guilt, and low self-esteem. Some believe that **low self-esteem is Satan's deadliest psychological weapon.** Low self-esteem has kept many disciples in "vicious circles of fear and uselessness."[6] Just recently, I heard a teenager say that she worries about everything every day. I related to her and had empathy for her since I too was constantly plagued with worry. Satan had used all of his psychological weapons against me. I couldn't even tell which one he used the most. Many times, I felt that I had insufficient self-esteem. Despite earning two master's degrees, I didn't feel smart enough or good enough. On the other hand, many times I felt the opposite, that I was "too much." Despite being a disciple, for eighteen years there was a constant internal conflict and insecurity that only subsided after I worked through many issues with a licensed psychologist. We were able to process my parents' separation and divorce, my father's emotional unavailability, a middle school assault, dreams deferred, codependency, and perfectionism, among other issues.

Though we probably know Ephesians 6:10–12 (the armor of God) by heart, **we also need to understand the specifics of how Satan's spiritual forces have imprisoned us psychologically.** Sadly and unnecessarily, many disciples are far from being healed of our low self-esteem. My heart felt broken as just last night, a dear sister shared that many times she felt that she hated to even see herself in the mirror. Unfortunately, self-hate continues to plague many disciples.

REFLECTION:

Do you have knowledge of and effectively manage the negative impact of past events or do they control you? Do you process and manage your emotions or do you let them control you?

Perfectionism

In our group discussions, disciple after disciple shared that they felt that they were never good enough to make their parents, guardians, or mates happy. Many have taken childlike ideas of responsibility into their adult life. Despite intellectually understanding that we did not cause our parents' divorce, our mother's alcoholism, our father's drug addition, being sent to a family member to be raised, an unpredictable home situation, or unwanted sexual abuse, we can maintain those flawed feelings of responsibility. God has called us to unload *all* of this. In Matthew 11:28–30 Jesus implores us, "Come to me, all you who are weary and burdened, and I will give you rest. Take my yoke upon you and learn from me, for I am gentle and humble in heart, and you *will find rest for your souls.* For my yoke is easy and my burden is light" (emphasis added). **Perfectionism is far too heavy a burden for anyone to bear, and it is not God's plan!**

Reaching Out

Without a doubt, what's most encouraging to me about the individuals who have invested in this healing process in discussion and support groups is that not only are we being healed, but we are becoming equipped to help heal others! The more I talk about growing up with an alcoholic stepfather and being assaulted, the more I see that I am not alone. Dealing with my own past hurts has helped me to have compassion for and a greater understanding of other people. If I hadn't experienced the things I did, I don't think that I would care as much for hurting people. It is amazing to me that God can change hurtful insights into healed and helpful outreach. I know that God will use my healing process to help others find healing. Many of the women in the groups are now able to encourage others in their efforts to be healthier and more mature emotionally and spiritually. Amen that God continues to help us in our weaknesses.

> We know that the whole creation has been groaning as in the pains of childbirth right up to the present time. Not only so, but we ourselves, who have the firstfruits of the Spirit, groan inwardly as we wait eagerly for our adoption to sonship, the redemption of our bodies.
>
> In the same way, the *Spirit helps us in our weakness.* We do not know what we ought to pray for, but the Spirit himself intercedes for us through wordless groans. And he who searches our hearts knows the mind of the Spirit, because the Spirit intercedes for God's people in accordance with the will of God.
>
> And we know that in all things God works for the good of those who love him, who have been called according to his purpose (Romans 8:22–23, 26–28, emphasis added).

REFLECTION:

What new convictions have you gained from this chapter? How do you want to enhance your relationship with God? What decision(s) would be helpful in your efforts to be transformed into the likeness of Jesus Christ (Romans 8:29)?

Chapter Four

My Personal Heroes: Courage and Healing

Running from problems is a race that we will never win.

—Source unknown

So many people are afraid of dealing with their emotional health issues. Many do not feel that they have the strength or the competence to effectively address issues that have been strongholds in their lives. And it is hard—if anyone tells you that healing or recovery is easy, they are not telling the truth. Repentance and recovery are every day, complicated, draining, complex, and multidimensional processes that deal with all of the aspects of our being: spiritual, emotional, mental, and physical. One goal as Christians is that we will make the profound changes that are necessary for healing our hearts and souls. This growth and eventual healing will take determination, focus, resources, and commitment.

This being true, obviously, fear can limit our potential for being all that God has planned for us. Brian Tracy is a specialist on the development of the human potential. He encourages us to control our fear, confront our fear, and do the thing that we fear in order to develop courage. Mark Twain wrote, "Courage is resistance to fear, mastery of fear—not absence of fear." Healing and recovery require that we act, move forward, and grow in spite of our fear.

I still remember a friend, Tracina Holland, encouraging our Spelman (Atlanta, Georgia) campus ministry to see challenges as opportunities to grow. We can treat every fear-inducing situation as a challenge and thus as an opportunity to transform our lives, minds, hearts, and souls. The only way to have victory over our strongholds is to do what we fear. If you fear going to counseling, a book discussion group, or a support group; confronting an abuser; eliminating unhealthy and unsafe people from your life, or standing up for yourself—do those things!

Brian Tracy's third rule for growth is: "Do the thing you fear and the death of fear is certain."[1] Can you think of when this process worked for you in your past, perhaps in the realm of public speaking, playing a sport, participating in a competition, approaching a stranger, or leading a Bible study? As the courageous testimonies that follow show, we can overcome our fears when we attack our fears.

REFLECTION:

When have you pushed past fears to accomplish a goal?

_____

_____

_____

What current fears do you need to face with courage?

_____

_____

_____

Not only can and should we use commonly proven techniques for overcoming fear, in God we have the most awesome power supporting and guiding us. He is our deliverance, power, and glory!

> Therefore, I urge you, brothers and sisters, in view of God's mercy, to offer your bodies as a living sacrifice, holy and pleasing to God—this is your true and proper worship. Do not conform to the pattern of this world, but *be transformed* by the renewing of your mind. Then you will be able to test and approve what God's will is—his good, pleasing and perfect will. (Romans 12:1-2, emphasis added).

For the eyes of the LORD range throughout the earth to strengthen those whose hearts are fully committed to him (2 Chronicles 16:9).

"I look for your deliverance, LORD" (Genesis 49:18).

Moses answered the people, "Do not be afraid. Stand firm and you will see the deliverance the LORD will bring you today. The Egyptians you see today you will never see again" (Exodus 14:13).

Then Hannah prayed and said:

"My heart rejoices in the Lord;
     in the Lord my horn is lifted high.
My mouth boasts over my enemies,
     for I delight in your deliverance" (1 Samuel 2:1).

When the LORD saw that they humbled themselves, this word of the LORD came to Shemaiah: "Since they have humbled themselves, I will not destroy them but will soon give them deliverance. My wrath will not be poured out on Jerusalem through Shishak" (2 Chronicles 12:7).

"You will not have to fight this battle. Take up your positions; stand firm and see the deliverance the LORD will give you, Judah and Jerusalem. Do not be afraid; do not be discouraged. Go out to face them tomorrow, and the LORD will be with you" (2 Chronicles 20:17).

"For if you remain silent at this time, relief and deliverance for the Jews will arise from another place, but you and your father's family will perish. And who knows but that you have come to your royal position for such a time as this?" (Esther 4:14).

"Indeed, this will turn out for my deliverance" (Job 13:16).

> But all the descendants of Israel
> will find deliverance in the LORD
> and will make their boast in him (Isaiah 45:25).

> For I know that through your prayers and God's provision of
> the Spirit of Jesus Christ what has happened to me will turn
> out for my deliverance (Philippians 1:19).

My personal heroes, whose testimonies I will share in this and upcoming chapters, have had the courage to change and also to realize that we are all "works in progress." For many of us, relationships come easy, we enjoy fellowship, and we have no problems praying and studying our Bibles every day. For others, these activities are severe challenges that are a consistent fight to accomplish. These fighting and courageous friends are my heroes! I hope and pray that you too will be encouraged by their daily decisions to allow God to transform their lives and to provide healing and deliverance. In order to protect personal privacy, names of those who have provided testimonies have been changed.

Sophia's Testimony

From depressed and out of touch...
to healing through humility, self-love, and self-knowledge

Attending the healing support group was the beginning of my healing process. As I answered and discussed the questions throughout and at the back of the *Healing for Damaged Emotions Workbook*, I began to deal with buried emotions. After a few meetings, I realized that I needed to seek professional help. My licensed counselor led me to discover that I have both depression and anxiety disorder.

Through counseling, the book discussion, and additional reading, I also realized that deepening self-knowledge creates power. I embraced the time I spent with my therapist as we talked through past issues that still affect me. One of the most important things I learned was that I had been out of touch with my feelings for most of my life. When I failed to acknowledge and effectively process my emotions, especially when I felt hurt, angered, and ignored, those emotions dictated how I related to God, others, and myself. Though I always knew God's truths in his word, the buried emotions many times were more powerful than that head knowledge.

Unfortunately, despite emotions being a God-given aspect of every human, I believe that talking about feelings and emotions is not a common practice. Some people feel uncomfortable when others are in touch with and talk about their feelings. This is especially true within the community where I grew up. Though no one stated the rules for emotions, I was implicitly expected to hide mine, especially those that were considered negative. I had to conform to the customs and values of my society, despite the result of giving up my true self. I could not show any anger, but had to hide it with a smile because anger was considered bad. Thus it was a surprise to me when I learned that the Bible does not consider angry feelings sin, but that reacting to those feelings of anger in an unrighteous way is considered sin.

I believe that God has allowed me to have anxiety and depression for my own good. His love has become more real to me in the moments when I feel hopelessness, guilt, and emotional pain. His constant forgiveness enables me to forgive others who have and who will hurt me.

Forgiveness is truly needed in order for damaged emotions to be healed. As God constantly forgives me and renews his grace on a daily basis, I must constantly forgive myself and others. I can easily condemn myself and thus do the same with others. I hold on to Romans 8:1: "Therefore, there is now no condemnation for those who are in Christ Jesus," and to Matthew 18:21–35. These scriptures help me to get to a place where I can forgive myself and others. God's teaching about forgiving and loving self has been one of the most profound revelations for me. I now know that I can only love others as much as I love myself. Jesus said in Luke 10:27, "Love the Lord your God with all your heart and with all your soul and with all your strength and with all your mind'; and 'Love your neighbor as yourself.'"

Additionally, I believe that healing is not possible without humility. God is able to use anything and anyone to help us heal, just as in the story about Naaman (2 Kings 5:1–14). For me, taking medicine for my depression and anxiety should not be an option because of the possible side effects. Yet, my condition worsened to the point that I had no other choice but to take medicine. I had to rely on God, trusting him and following the advice of my doctors and the therapist God has placed in my life. After much prayer, I finally found a doctor who prescribed the combination of medicines that work for me. With the doctor's directives, I feel so much better. I realized that I never knew what "normal" felt like until I began taking the medication. I also found that I did not need to be on medication for life. As I learned how to deal with my depressive symptoms, I was able to stop taking medication and began to use alternative practices.

Chapter Five

Spiritual Foundation

In consideration of Mark 8:36, "What good is it for someone to gain the whole world, yet forfeit their soul?" we must always keep in mind that our relationship with God and the salvation of our souls is our absolute first priority. All of our work towards having healthy hearts and emotions must be built on a strong and biblical spiritual foundation.

Although God has brought us to him in many different ways, as disciples of Christ many of us are extremely blessed to have come to an educated decision regarding our faith through the study series commonly used within our fellowship, titled in various congregations *First Principles,*[1] *Shining Like Stars,*[2] or *Equipping,* among other titles. These topical Bible studies develop the spiritual foundation that all Christians need. Disciples recall that the experience of processing and applying the Scriptures and the relationships built while studying these fundamental teachings were both invaluable. We believe that our relationship with God, discipleship, and the biblical principles learned through the study series are the foundation for everything in our lives. Without this foundation, all else could be labeled a "chasing after the wind"—a mere waste of time (Ecclesiastes 1:14).

Come along as I think back on what we learned. During our initial Bible studies, we made a number of educated decisions. If we hadn't already, we decided to seek God with all of our heart, mind, soul, and strength. We may have studied scriptures on Jesus and grace. For sure, we studied about the Bible being the authoritative word of God and made the decision to have God's word as the standard for our lives. Without that decision, we would not have had a chance to become Christians. We then learned the Bible's definition of disciple, or Christian. This was so important because if we take a poll of ten people, we just may end up with ten different definitions of what it means to be a Christian. We are so grateful for the disciples who sacrificed time, energy, gas, and more to share about God's exciting purpose and mission for all of his children.

Though we all pretty much knew that rape and adultery were wrong, many of us were a bit shocked to see lists of sins in the Bible such as those in Mark 7, Galatians 5, and 2 Timothy 3. It was encouraging when disciples shared their stories: the good and bad, and the ugly sins they had committed. Personalizing the ways we'd hurt God with our sins of commission and omission led to the convictions we needed in order to repent and become Christians. The realization that our sins actually separate us from God (Isaiah 59:1–2) woke many of us up to our alarming spiritual realities.

REFLECTION:

Are you continually studying the Bible to apply it to your life? Do you understand what God's purpose and mission are for your life and the Bible verses that delineate both?

_____

_____

_____

We praised and thanked God when we studied the cross of Christ and began to understand the depth of God's love and Jesus' personal sacrifices. We remain committed to God today because of our understanding of the crucifixion. We remember reading the medical account of what Jesus suffered physically for us. How powerful! Though Mel Gibson received tons of criticism about his movie, *The Passion of Christ*[3] was the closest many of us have ever seen to what Jesus actually suffered as a result of our sins and for our forgiveness. God's sacrificial love is still pretty unfathomable! (Matthew 26–27). Amen that on a daily basis we can make the decision to die to sins and live for righteousness (1 Peter 2:21–25). God is so gracious!

Who of us had not heard that repentance is confession? How great it was to learn the actual definition of the word and the biblical meaning of repentance! Many of us desperately wanted to change and live for God but didn't know how. Nor did we have the power of God's Spirit to do so. Some of us had "accepted Jesus as our Savior" as many times as the doors of the church were opened, but never really had a significant change in our behavior or our understanding of God's attitude toward sin. Then some of the best news we ever heard came as we learned of God's plan for the forgiveness of our sins through baptism (Acts 2:38, Acts 8, 1 Peter 3:21, Romans 6:3–4, Colossians 2:12, Matthew 28:19, and Acts 22:16). The idea that all of our sins (we each wrote our personal list of them) could be totally wiped out was absolutely unbelievable. God's grace is utterly amazing!

REFLECTION:

Have you ever studied out the sins that separate you from God; your sins that Jesus died for? If so, how long ago? Have you ever looked up the definition of repentance and studied it in the Bible? Have you ever read a medical account of the crucifixion? How did it impact you?

_____

_____

_____

Our studies would not have been complete and we could not have made an educated decision without taking a look at the varied teachings on how to become a Christian. Again, if we polled ten people on what the Bible says about how to become a Christian, we probably would get at least ten different answers. But we know that God's word doesn't change and that we are not to preach a "different gospel" (Galatians 1:6–9).

Unfortunately, some of us have seen, heard, or been a part of horror stories in churches. It was sometimes hard to see God amidst all of the sin, church fights, church splits, and confusion. Many of us grew up in dysfunctional and sinful families and churches. It might have been hard to admit that our sins had even damaged God's perfect plan for his church. The study of his plan for the church was encouraging and inspiring. Despite our own sinfulness, God planned for us to become a part of his family, the church. What a blessing and honor. We learned that Jesus is the head of the body and that we are members of the body (Colossians 1:18 and 1 Corinthians 12). Though we felt that we had so much to learn, we were also excited about how we could give to one another and help each other make it to heaven (Hebrews 3:12–13 and 10:24–25). What an example the early church is for us to follow! (Acts 2).

Then, finally, as we made a decision to commit our lives and our all to Jesus, we counted the cost. Many of us read what Paul wrote in 1 Corinthians 15:1–2:

> Now, brothers and sisters, I want to remind you of the gospel I preached to you, which you received and on which you have taken your stand. By this gospel you are saved, if you hold firmly to the word I preached to you. Otherwise, you have believed in vain.

We were also called to consider if we would be committed to God for the rest of our lives. Then, knowing that God was providing all we needed and that grace saves us and would carry us until we die or Christ comes back—we took the plunge! We were baptized for the forgiveness of our sins. Those of you who took this journey: Remember the feeling? Remember the joy? Remember the clarity? Remember the gratitude? Remember the commitment to be willing to go anywhere, do anything, and give up everything since God has done that for us? When was the last time you told your story to someone? God's power is seen through the amazing changes he made in each of our lives. Let's encourage each other with our conversion stories and our continued efforts to become all the more like Christ.

If you are reading this book and have not yet had the opportunity to work through the study series I just described, I encourage you to find a fellowship close to you (on the www.disciplestoday.org Church Locator page), make the call, and begin the greatest journey ever!

REFLECTION:

Do you attend a church fellowship where people have made educated decisions to have the Bible as the standard for their lives and to live as disciples in a love relationship with God? Is the church you attend a reflection of the New Testament church? Does your fellowship reflect the diversity of your country's population?

My Christian Story

I grew up attending a Baptist church in North East Washington DC and other Baptist churches in Philadelphia and Greensboro and Mc-Cleansville, North Carolina. When I turned sixteen and was able to work at a McDonalds in a Greensboro mall, I rarely attended services. Due to my family circumstances, I was determined to have money of my own. Though I was and am eternally and extremely grateful for the foundation of faith that was provided as I heard the amazing stories of God, Jesus, Abraham, Isaac, and Jacob, I found very little practical teaching or spiritual relationships that could help me to deal with peer pressure, decision making, my parents separating and divorcing, an alcoholic stepfather, and other issues. I believed in God, wanted to do what was right, tried to be a "good person," and felt that because of these values and convictions, I would definitely make it to heaven. At the same time, I did not know how to deal with the many internal conflicts and the sadness that we often experience in our development. Many times, I attempted to read the Bible, but I seldom studied it. Though I was considered intelligent, I had serious problems understanding the Elizabethan English used in the King James Version. In Job 30:27 the KJV says, "My bowels boiled, and rested not: the days of affliction prevented me." I so appreciate the folks who introduced me to the New International Version and additional, more current translations of the Bible. I understand "The churning inside me never stops; days of suffering confront me."

God had a plan to meet my needs and help me know him, his love, and his purpose for my life. Though I had always planned to return to Philadelphia to attend Temple University, God had another plan. A volleyball coach from the University of North Carolina at Charlotte saw me play during a high school game. I had never thought about playing in college, but accepted the opportunity and changed plans. We had "boot camp" before school started...no one could call it practice. It was more like torture. Hardly any of us could walk after the first day. Unfortunately, I suffered a knee injury, had an operation (to reattach my cartilage), and spent three months in a cast from my hip to my ankle. Though I was highly disappointed, my father expressed gratitude for the doctor and the cast. He didn't want me to return to playing and have my knee lock up while jumping to spike the ball.

I met many people as a result of the cast and crutches. One morning, as I waited for campus police transportation, Betty Herbert asked me if I needed assistance. I didn't, but we talked for a bit and she invited me to visit her church. I was shocked, to say the least, because Betty is Caucasian. I surely was not aware of any interracial churches in North Carolina during the mid-80s. I later visited and could only sit on the floor (with a red skirt), since the folding chairs would not accommodate an angled cast. I was blown away by the love expressed in the relationships I saw. More impactful was the members' desire and ability to answer my questions with scriptures. I was used to hearing all kinds of varying opinions, but I was not accustomed to seeing people who lived with the Bible as the standard for every aspect of their lives rather than traditions, emotions, leaders, or anything else.

I began to study the Bible with new friends from the Charlotte, North Carolina fellowship. I was so excited about the things I was learning that I invited friends to come to my studies. I guess I didn't remember or wasn't told that the studies were for me personally! To this day, I am grateful for Martha (Ann) and Debbie who took the time to share with me the truths of God's word and their lives. For me today, that is one of the greatest joys I have: sharing God's word with others. He has changed me and my life completely!

REFLECTION:

How do your relationships help you on a practical level to live in accordance with God's word? Can you back up your spiritual beliefs with specific scriptures? How often do you use God's word to teach, correct, rebuke, and train yourself and fellow believers?

Alexandra's Testimony

From sexually abused and inwardly conflicted...
to healing of past traumas in God's comforting presence

I was a single mom and disciple for fifteen years when given the opportunity to participate in a local emotional healing group discussion. In theory, it sounded good. However, after I committed and as the first meeting approached, I found myself wrestling with thoughts concerning why it was not a good idea to participate. I didn't want to rehash old issues, I didn't know the people who would be in the group, and I didn't want to expose my inner turmoil to anyone else. I also didn't want to form friendships that would only last during the group sessions. I kept wondering why I wanted to join such a group in the first place.

Then it dawned on me that God knows me (Psalm 139) and he knows what's going on inside me. I realized that I was afraid and (since I am a visual person) I pictured myself standing on the threshold of the fear of revealing things to others and confronting issues never discussed. I had a choice to make: I could continue to be haunted and "damaged" or I could allow God to show me something different. I chose to try. It was not easy.

At each meeting we discussed and worked on assignments from one or two previously read chapters. Chapter 4 ("Satan's Deadliest Weapons") of David Seamands' *Healing for Damaged Emotions* enabled me to see from a perspective that was different from mine and it empowered me to see that God is real and that he has a plan for the ugliest situations. Many who joined the discussions, for various reasons, were not able to complete the workbook. I did and I'm happy that God gave me the courage to go to each meeting. The discussions were the first step in the plan God had for me to heal wounds that existed deep within. He wanted to heal even the pain that only he knew. I wasn't miraculously healed overnight, but God made it clear to me that I was not forgotten, I wasn't ruined, and I had a purpose in the exact state that I was in.

Though I shared with the group that I was sexually assaulted, it wasn't until our last meeting (after thirteen months) that I was able to share that it was actually my father who was the assailant. Not only did he abuse me sexually, but he was horribly physically abusive to my mother. The safe environment in our discussion group allowed me to have that breakthrough!

I now have confidence that God loves me. I trust that he will teach me what I do not yet understand. I smile when I think of God. I am so grateful for his love, compassion, and mercy. He continues to hold my hand through my journey, and I've learned the comfort of leaving my burdens and pain with him, allowing him to lead me.

Chapter Six

Dig a Little Deeper:
Wisdom and Emotional Health

Surely you desire truth in the inner parts;
    you teach me wisdom in the inmost place (Psalm 51:6 NIV 1984).

The purposes of a person's heart are deep waters,
    but one who has insight draws them out (Proverbs 20:5).

Though heart and soul (character) work is not easy, its benefits far outweigh the effort. Unless we really know ourselves, we won't know our needs in our relationship with God, our relationship with ourselves, or our relationships with others. After ten years of professional counseling, I'm still digging, still working to align my emotions and emotional reactions with God's will. After eighteen years of earnestly working on the actions of being a disciple, it was great to begin to really focus more on the deeper, heart and soul issues of being like Jesus. In this chapter we're going to learn a bit from the work of some great authors, but first let's look to the movies.

I'm a big movie buff and am not ashamed to admit that some of my favorites are Disney animated films. One of my recent favorites is *The Princess and the Frog*.[1] The song "Dig a Little Deeper," sung by the character Mama Odie, performed by Jenifer Lewis and featuring the Pinnacle Gospel Choir, really struck a chord in me. Mama Odie encourages the princess to not be superficial, to dig a little and focus on heart and soul.

I love how Mama Odie sang about blue skies and sunshine. It made me think about Acts 3:19: "Repent, then, and turn to God, so that your sins may be wiped out, that times of refreshing may come from the Lord." We can all continue to work on learning, digging, changing, and growing in our emotional maturity. As we do, we will witness those times of continued spiritual and emotional refreshing. I hope you'll continue with me on this amazing journey!

REFLECTION:

Do you feel that you have been able to go beyond changing your external behaviors to a focus on knowing and growing in your heart and soul? In what ways have you dug deeper?

_____

_____

_____

The Emotionally Healthy Church

In his book, *The Emotionally Healthy Church*,[2] Peter Scazzero provides an Inventory of Spiritual/Emotional Maturity. Disciples have focused on spiritual health and can usually spot when someone is not doing well spiritually or is not spiritually mature. We, having believed the Bible, decided that it will be our standard for life. We committed to living lives of discipleship, being "born again" (John 3) and enjoying the power of God's Spirit to help us in our daily walk as Christians.

And yet, not enough disciples have given deep and continual consideration to emotional health and maturity. After years of counseling and a continued focus on healing and being healthy emotionally, I'm excited about being "born again" emotionally! Has your discipleship impacted the emotional components of your life? I encourage you to take the Inventory of Spiritual/Emotional Maturity in Scazzero's book or on his website, (http://www.emotionallyhealthy.org/). He defines, describes, and interprets four levels of emotional maturity. From his inventory, we can determine if we are emotional adults, adolescents, children, or infants. It may also be helpful to share your inventory results with a close friend for their feedback and support.

As I mentioned before, disciples have worked long and hard at being mature spiritually. We have read the scripture about living on milk as an infant versus the constant use of solid food and training that lead us to maturity (Hebrews 5:11–14). My hope and prayer is that we can increase our capacity to be mature spiritually by growing emotionally. These two are intrinsically connected. We can't have one without the other. Though many of us have grown beyond the emotional infant stage, we may still be an adolescent or child emotionally. One full-time minister shared that he was shocked that the inventory classified him as an emotional child. Let's all work on growing toward emotional adulthood.

REFLECTION:

Have you felt stuck in any areas of your life? Have you considered seeking assistance from a professional counselor to help you break through in those areas?

Emotional Intelligence

Emotional intelligence (EQ) has been found to be a predictor of professional and relationship success. Though IQ and personality style contribute to our performance, they are fairly static. On the other hand, the good news is that emotional intelligence skills can be developed. EQ is also the foundation for many soft skills such as stress, time, anger and relationship management. One of my favorite EQ quotes is by Aristotle. Daniel Goleman reports that in the *Nicomachean Ethics*, Aristotle states that "anyone can become angry—that is easy. But to be angry with the right person, to the right degree, at the right time, for the right purpose, and in the right way—that is not easy." This can apply to many of our emotions and feelings.

Dr. Goleman published a #1 Best Seller, *Emotional Intelligence: Why It Can Matter More than IQ*, in 1996 and then again in 2006. He lists the fundamentals of emotional intelligence as self-awareness, self-management, social awareness, and the ability to manage relationships. He notes that emotional competencies are learned abilities. Dr. Goleman's goal in his book is to help us understand emotional intelligence and how to "bring intelligence to our emotions."[3] He discusses how our emotional habits can undermine our best intentions and how our emotional impulses can be self-defeating. I appreciate the effort Dr. Goleman gives to showing us how to become more emotionally intelligent. It is akin to God's exhortation to not merely look into the mirror of his word but to do what it says (James 1:22–25).

The *Oxford English Dictionary*[4] defines emotion as "any agitation or disturbance of mind, feeling, passion; any vehement or excited mental state." Daniel Goleman defines emotion as a feeling and its distinctive thoughts, psychological and biological states, and range of propensities to act. He provides a list of core emotions (such as anger, sadness, fear, joy, and love) and their families.

As we explore this important God-given part of our being and strive to increase our emotional intelligence and self-awareness, it may be good for many of us who previously paid little attention to our emotions to keep a "feelings journal." One of the first assignments given by my counselor was that of journaling the emotions I recognized on a daily basis. I had suppressed my emotions for far too long. I actually needed a list of emotions placed on the first page of my journal to help. Each day I would read over the list asking myself if I felt any of those things. Socrates' injunction "Know thyself" speaks to the keystone of emotional intelligence: awareness of one's own feelings as they occur. God encourages us all to examine ourselves and have a sober judgment of ourselves (1 Corinthians 11 and Romans 12). It's taken a good amount of time for me to reverse the eighteen years of attempting to ignore my emotions. I encourage you to explore your emotions in a similar way. Since our brain processes stimulants in the limbic system *before* information reaches our rational brain, we feel things before we assign meaning to them and process them. Without EQ, there is limited self-control. **Either we know, understand, and manage our emotions, or they control us.** In order to be healthy spiritually and emotionally, we must know ourselves.

The Bible on Wisdom and Knowledge

We can learn a lot from books, and of course, the word of God teaches us about our emotions. As we explore emotional intelligence, it is important to pray for God's support, direction, revelation, strength, and wisdom. James noted that the "desires that battle within" us cause fights and quarrels (James 4:1–3). He then says that we do not have because we do not ask God. We can avoid living as less than an emotional adult by praying for emotional intelligence, knowledge, and wisdom. I like to explore the definitions of words to see if it will lead me to a deeper understanding or a different perspective. We all have ideas about what wisdom and knowledge are, but let's look at the definitions.

Wisdom is defined as the quality or state of being wise; having the power of discerning and judging properly as to what is true or right; knowledge of what is true or right coupled with just judgment as to action; sagacity, discernment, or insight. Wisdom also means having knowledge or information as to facts, circumstances, etc. Knowledge is defined as an acquaintance with facts, truths, or principles, as from study or investigation.

As Christians, our number one goal is to intimately know God. In addition, knowing and understanding ourselves is necessary for an intimate relationship with God and the ability to love and minister to others with pure motivations. Self- and social/relational knowledge and understanding are paramount as we navigate our world.

Below are a number of scriptures that show

- God's desire for us to have knowledge and wisdom
- Our forefathers' prayers for knowledge and wisdom
- The cost of not attaining knowledge and wisdom
- God's plan for us to gain knowledge and wisdom

Wisdom and Knowledge

The fear of the LORD is the beginning of knowledge,
    but fools despise wisdom and instruction (Proverbs 1:7).

The mocker seeks wisdom and finds none,
    but knowledge comes easily to the discerning (Proverbs 14:6).

The discerning heart seeks knowledge,
    but the mouth of a fool feeds on folly (Proverbs 15:14).

Desire without knowledge is not good—
    how much more will hasty feet miss the way! (Proverbs 19:2).

Flog a mocker, and the simple will learn prudence;
    rebuke the discerning, and they will gain knowledge
                         (Proverbs 19:25).

Gold there is, and rubies in abundance,
    but lips that speak knowledge are a rare jewel (Proverbs 20:15).

Apply your heart to instruction
    and your ears to words of knowledge (Proverbs 23:12).

For I can testify about them that they are zealous for God, but their zeal is not based on knowledge (Romans 10:2).

Coral and jasper are not worthy of mention;
    the price of wisdom is beyond rubies (Job 28:18).

My son, do not forget my teaching,
    but keep my commands in your heart (Proverbs 3:1).

Get wisdom, get understanding;
    do not forget my words or turn away from them (Proverbs 4:5).

Wisdom is supreme; therefore get wisdom.
    Though it cost all you have, get understanding (Proverbs 4:7).

Wisdom is more precious than rubies,
    and nothing you desire can compare with her (Proverbs 8:11).

"I, wisdom, dwell together with prudence;
    I possess knowledge and discretion" (Proverbs 8:12).

A fool finds pleasure in wicked schemes,
    but a person of understanding delights in wisdom (Proverbs 10:23).

The wisdom of the prudent is to give thought to their ways,
    but the folly of fools is deception (Proverbs 14:8).

Wisdom reposes in the heart of the discerning
and even among fools she lets herself be known (Proverbs
14:33).

The one who gets wisdom loves his life;
the one who cherishes understanding will soon prosper
(Proverbs 19:8).

We do, however, speak a message of wisdom among the mature,
but not the wisdom of this age or of the rulers of this age, who
are coming to nothing (1 Corinthians 2:6).

We need to thoroughly and deeply know ourselves! We all need to have the knowledge and wisdom needed for emotional and spiritual maturity. We have to dig a little deeper. God has implored us to love him with all our *heart, mind, soul,* and *strength.* As you read his words, please consider how you can apply his thoughts on wisdom and knowledge to your emotional life, health, and quest for greater levels of maturity.

REFLECTION:

Have you ever interacted with a very zealous person who did not have the knowledge to back up their zeal (Romans 10:12)? Would you consider this zealous person safe spiritually?

_____

_____

_____

What have you done to increase knowledge about your ways, the impact of past traumatic events, your tendencies and patterns in interpersonal relationships, and your heart and soul?

_____

Wisdom and Knowledge Prayers

In our personal relationship with God, we can learn from, meditate on, and even incorporate some of the prayers we find in his word.

"Give me wisdom and knowledge, that I may lead this people, for who is able to govern this great people of yours?"

God said to Solomon, "Since this is your heart's desire and you have not asked for wealth, possessions or honor, nor for the death of your enemies, and since you have not asked for a long life but for wisdom and knowledge to govern my people over whom I have made you king, therefore wisdom and knowledge will be given you. And I will also give you wealth, possessions and honor, such as no king who was before you ever had and none after you will have" (2 Chronicles 1:10–12).

Teach me knowledge and good judgment,
for I trust your commands (Psalm 119:66).

And this is my prayer: that your love may abound more and more in knowledge and depth of insight (Philippians 1:9).

For this reason, since the day we heard about you, we have not stopped praying for you. We continually ask God to fill you with the knowledge of his will through all the wisdom and understanding that the Spirit gives, so that you may live a life worthy of the Lord and please him in every way: bearing fruit in every good work, growing in the knowledge of God (Colossians 1:9–10).

Teach us to number our days,
that we may gain a heart of wisdom (Psalm 90:12).

"I thank and praise you, God of my ancestors:

You have given me wisdom and power,
you have made known to me what we asked of you,
you have made known to us the dream of the king" (Daniel 2:23).

I keep asking that the God of our Lord Jesus Christ, the glorious Father, may give you the Spirit of wisdom and revelation, so that you may know him better (Ephesians 1:17).

REFLECTION:

In addition to the results from Peter Scazzero's Inventory of Spiritual/ Emotional Maturity, how would you rate yourself regarding your depth of insight, spiritual wisdom, and understanding? Are you typically able to understand issues beyond the surface presentations people give?

_____

_____

_____

How does Paul say we can live a life worthy of the Lord and please him?

_____

_____

_____

Can you give examples of when God and Jesus showed their emotions? How many people in the Bible can you list who were "angry with God"? Do they exhibit what Aristotle described regarding the appropriateness of emotions (degree, time, purpose, way)?

_____

_____

Wisdom and Knowledge Results

"But if they do not listen,
	they will perish by the sword
	and die without knowledge" (Job 36:12).

The wise store up knowledge,
	but the mouth of a fool invites ruin (Proverbs 10:14).

With their mouths the godless destroy their neighbors,
	but through knowledge the righteous escape (Proverbs 11:9).

All who are prudent act with knowledge,
	but fools expose their folly (Proverbs 13:16).

The simple inherit folly,
	but the prudent are crowned with knowledge (Proverbs 14:18).

The lips of the wise spread knowledge;
	but the hearts of fools are not upright (Proverbs 15:7).

Stop listening to instruction, my son,
	and you will stray from the words of knowledge (Proverbs 19:27).

The wise prevail through great power,
	and those who have knowledge muster their strength
						(Proverbs 24:5).

Israel's watchmen are blind,
	they all lack knowledge;
they are all mute dogs,
	they cannot bark;
they lie around and dream,
	they love to sleep (Isaiah 56:10).

"My people are destroyed from lack of knowledge.
    Because you have rejected knowledge,
I also reject you as my priests;
    because you have ignored the law of your God,
I also will ignore your children" (Hosea 4:6).

Furthermore, just as they did not think it worthwhile to retain the knowledge of God, so God gave them over to a depraved mind, so that they do what ought not to be done (Romans 1:28).

"Your servant Joab did this to change the present situation. My lord has wisdom like that of an angel of God—he knows everything that happens in the land" (2 Samuel 14:20).

The LORD gave Solomon wisdom, just as he had promised him. There were peaceful relations between Hiram and Solomon, and the two of them made a treaty (1 Kings 5:12).

The mouths of the righteous utter wisdom,
    and their tongues speak what is just (Psalm 37:30).

My son, if you accept my words
    and store up my commands within you,
turning your ear to wisdom
    and applying your heart to understanding—
indeed, if you call out for insight
    and cry aloud for understanding,
and if you look for it as for silver
    and search for it as for hidden treasure,
then you will understand the fear of the LORD
    and find the knowledge of God.
For the Lord gives wisdom;
    from his mouth come knowledge and understanding
                                            (Proverbs 2:1–6).

For wisdom will enter your heart,

and knowledge will be pleasant to your soul (Proverbs 2:10).
Wisdom will save you from the ways of wicked men,
     from men whose words are perverse (Proverbs 2:12).

Blessed are those who find wisdom,
     those who gain understanding (Proverbs 3:13).

Do not forsake wisdom, and she will protect you;
     love her, and she will watch over you (Proverbs 4:6).

If you are wise, your wisdom will reward you;
     if you are a mocker, you alone will suffer (Proverbs 9:12).

Wisdom is found on the lips of the discerning,
     but a rod is for the back of one who has no sense
                                        (Proverbs 10:13).

When pride comes, then comes disgrace,
     but with humility comes wisdom (Proverbs 11:2).

A man is praised according to his wisdom,
     but men with warped minds are despised (Proverbs 12:8).

Where there is strife, there is pride,
     but wisdom is found in those who take advice (Proverbs 13:10).

The mocker seeks wisdom and finds none,
     but knowledge comes easily to the discerning (Proverbs 14:6).

A person's wisdom yields patience;
     it is to one's glory to overlook an offense (Proverbs 19:11).

Know also that wisdom is like honey for you:
     If you find it, there is a future hope for you,
     and your hope will not be cut off (Proverbs 24:14).

Those who trust in themselves are fools,

but those who walk in wisdom are kept safe (Proverbs 28:26).
Wisdom, like an inheritance, is a good thing
    and benefits those who see the sun (Ecclesiastes 7:11).

Wisdom is a shelter
    as money is a shelter,
but the advantage of knowledge is this:
    Wisdom preserves those who have it (Ecclesiastes 7:12).

Wisdom makes one wise person more powerful
    than ten rulers in a city (Ecclesiastes 7:19).

Who is like the wise?
    Who knows the explanation of things?
A person's wisdom brightens their face
    and changes its hard appearance (Ecclesiastes 8:1).

As dead flies give perfume a bad smell,
    so a little folly outweighs wisdom and honor (Ecclesiastes 10:1).

Who is wise and understanding among you? Let them show it by their good life, by deeds done in the humility that comes from wisdom (James 3:13).

REFLECTION:

What is the impact of a lack of wisdom and knowledge? Has your biblical knowledge impacted not only your behaviors but also your heart and soul?

_____

_____

_____

Which scriptures about the positive and negative results of wisdom stand out to you the most? Why? How important are self-awareness and self-management (EQ skills) to our spiritual health?

God's Plan for Gaining Wisdom and Knowledge

The LORD gives wisdom;
> from his mouth come knowledge and understanding
>> (Proverbs 2:6).

Wisdom will enter your heart,
> and knowledge will be pleasant to your soul (Proverbs 2:10).

Whoever loves discipline loves knowledge,
> but whoever hates correction is stupid (Proverbs 12:1).

The heart of the discerning acquires knowledge;
> the ears of the wise seek it out (Proverbs 18:15).

To the man who pleases him, God gives wisdom, knowledge and happiness, but to the sinner he gives the task of gathering and storing up wealth to hand it over to the one who pleases God (Ecclesiastes 2:26).

Wisdom is a shelter
> as money is a shelter,
but the advantage of knowledge is this:
> Wisdom preserves those who have it (Ecclesiastes 7:12).

"Then I will give you shepherds after my own heart, who will lead you with knowledge and understanding" (Jeremiah 3:15).

"He changes times and seasons;

  he deposes kings and raises up others.
He gives wisdom to the wise
  and knowledge to the discerning" (Daniel 2:21).

For God, who said, "Let light shine out of darkness," made his light shine in our hearts to give us the light of the knowledge of God's glory displayed in the face of Christ (2 Corinthians 4:6).

But since you excel in everything—in faith, in speech, in knowledge, in complete earnestness and in the love we have kindled in you—see that you also excel in this grace of giving (2 Corinthians 8:7).

We demolish arguments and every pretension that sets itself up against the knowledge of God, and we take captive every thought to make it obedient to Christ (2 Corinthians 10:5).

...and to know this love that surpasses knowledge—that you may be filled to the measure of all the fullness of God (Ephesians 3:19).

...until we all reach unity in the faith and in the knowledge of the Son of God and become mature, attaining to the whole measure of the fullness of Christ (Ephesians 4:13).

You...have put on the new self, which is being renewed in knowledge in the image of its Creator (Colossians 3:10).

...God our Savior, who wants all men to be saved and to come to a knowledge of the truth (1 Timothy 2:4).

His divine power has given us everything we need for a godly life through our knowledge of him who called us by his own glory and goodness (2 Peter 1:3).

For this very reason, make every effort to add to your faith goodness; and to goodness, knowledge; and to knowledge, self-control; and to self-control, perseverance; and to perseverance, godliness....

For if you possess these qualities in increasing measure, they will keep you from being ineffective and unproductive in your knowledge of our Lord Jesus Christ (2 Peter 1:5–6, 8).

But grow in the grace and knowledge of our Lord and Savior Jesus Christ. To him be glory both now and forever! Amen (2 Peter 3:18).

Surely you desire truth in the inner parts;
    you teach me wisdom in the inmost place (Psalm 51:6 NIV 1984).

With all wisdom and understanding, he made known to us the mystery of his will (Ephesians 1:8b–9a).

Such regulations indeed have an appearance of wisdom, with their self-imposed worship, their false humility and their harsh treatment of the body, but they lack any value in restraining sensual indulgence (Colossians 2:23).

If any of you lacks wisdom, you should ask God, who gives generously to all without finding fault, and it will be given to you (James 1:5).

But the wisdom that comes from heaven is first of all pure; then peace-loving, considerate, submissive, full of mercy and good fruit, impartial and sincere (James 3:17).

REFLECTION:

Which scriptures about God's plan for us to gain wisdom and knowledge stand out to you the most? Why?

_____

_____

_____

How important is it for us to know and understand ourselves? Why?

_____

_____

_____

Only after we've been able to clear out any emotional sewage and effectively process emotional damage (in our hearts and souls) are we able to replace it with wisdom, knowledge, love, and all the other good qualities. Have you been able to dispose of your emotional sewage? Have God's truths been able to reach your inner parts, the inmost places?

_____

_____

_____

Do you feel that you see yourself the way God sees you? Have you been able to take captive any automatic negative thoughts (those pesky ANTS) and feelings that do not reflect God's thoughts of you?

_____

_____

_____

Madison's Testimony
From feeling all alone without direction...
to healing through partners in personal growth and courage

My greatest struggles have been depression, not trusting God, and fear. Reading *Healing for Damaged Emotions* by David Seamands and Beth Funk and participating in the support group discussions have been a great aide for me during a time in my walk with God that has been the hardest yet. I have specifically worked on understanding and battling my greatest struggles.

The book has given me insight to many of the issues I am dealing with from a psychological and Christian perspective, which is what I've been longing for. The group provides a safe place for me to spill my thoughts—with no judgment and plenty of people who surprisingly can relate to some of my thoughts, experiences, and feelings.

I'm still working through understanding my "family-of-origin issues." I understand that my mom and grandmother were both overly cautious and very controlling. I understand that my father was distant and could have even been considered "absent" though we resided in the same home. Once my father left, it seemed that things fell apart with my mom. She seemed to be acutely depressed, as evidenced by the lack of keeping up the house and a disturbing increase of hoarding. This was also a turning point for me. I remember feeling more and more anxious and experiencing my first major depression. On top of my parents' separation, there were additional major transitions taking place at the same time. I was overloaded and found security and safety in being alone or just with my mom. I hated going out to any events, felt extremely fragile and scared, felt that no one understood me and that there was no one to protect me, and felt safer with adults. Unfortunately, I didn't understand grief and always felt that I was oversensitive. This made me turn inward all the more.

I had wanted to go to therapy for a while, but being part of the group helped me to really take that leap and seek further help. I was able to overcome my fears and benefit from a professional. The support I receive from our discussion group reminds me that I am not alone. It is especially comforting to feel that I can talk without feeling that everyone else is trying to "fix" me. Seamands' book covers so many important topics that people struggle with and that I personally struggle with, and provides helpful illustrations and examples of each topic. The questions in the book gave me direction. I would recommend it (and already have) and participation in a group discussion to anyone.

Chapter Seven

Numbing the Pain
and Repeating the Cycle

Insanity: doing the same thing over and over again and expecting different results. —*Source unknown*

"It is hard for you to kick against the goads" (Acts 26:14).

If you studied the Bible in depth as part of your journey to become a disciple, you probably talked about most of your significant life events at that time. Some of us erroneously believed that salvation would miraculously heal the pain of our past and fix our dysfunctional and self-sabotaging repetitive behaviors. When this miracle didn't occur, many of us tried praying more, reading more, studying with others more, fasting more, and getting more advice. It has been wonderful to see a growing number of disciples pursuing careers in counseling, yet at this time there remain relatively few trained and licensed psychologists in our fellowship. Psychologists know what many long-time disciples have come to understand: for some issues, prayer and Bible study alone won't heal the heart or "fix" the damage.

Instead of understanding the need to address these issues with the assistance of professional psychologists, many of us "grit it out" the best we can and end up suffering from many symptoms of damaged emotions. Gritting it out is like putting a Band-Aid on a gunshot wound, as it usually ends up being only a temporary fix to a problem that requires more in-depth attention. We can also turn to things that provide us with temporary relief at best, or sometimes we seek to escape the pain by turning to things that are addictive and even more harmful in the long run, including food, shopping, men, women, relationships, sex, pornography, fantasy novels, busyness, leadership, drama, chaos, worry, caretaking, over-functioning, exercising, religion, approval of others, medicine, drugs and alcohol, television, music, computer games, social networking, hobbies, sports, or work.

Obviously, there can be a lot of danger in turning to "things" to ease the pain that we feel inside, even things that are supposed to be good, such as serving others or volunteering. We have to be careful that we are not being outwardly focused in order to avoid focusing on our own character issues that need our serious attention. Self-reflection can be a good thing, but we may tell ourselves that thinking about ourselves and working on ourselves is selfish. Be wary of this trap!

REFLECTION:

Have you been excessive (debaucherous) in aspects of your life? If so, why? Are there any unhealthy patterns or generational cycles you repeat? If so, have you been able to figure out why? Is there something that you turn to in order to avoid dealing with what's going on deep in your heart?

_____

_____

_____

When we avoid dealing with our issues, we can become self-destructive. We can feel like we should be able to handle them on our own, or we tell ourselves that we are the only ones going through whatever it is we are going through and no one will be able to relate or to help. Contrary to this lie of Satan, we are not alone!

Destructive behaviors and paradigms, the opposite of God's life to the full (John 10:10), have existed in most of our lives. Eating disorders are just one example of such behaviors. The National Eating Disorders Association reports that there has been unprecedented growth in eating disorders in the past two decades. In the United States, 20 million women and ten million men suffer from a clinically significant eating disorder at some time in their life, including anorexia nervosa, bulimia nervosa, binge eating disorder, or an eating disorder not otherwise specified. The incidence of bulimia in 10- to 39-year-old women tripled between 1988 and 1993.[1]

It is also common for eating disorders to occur with one or more other psychiatric disorders, which can complicate treatment and make recovery more difficult. Among those who suffer from eating disorders:

- Alcohol and other substance abuse disorders are four times more common than in the general population.
- Depression and other mood disorders co-occur quite frequently.
- There is a markedly elevated risk for obsessive-compulsive disorder.

We further see these self-destructive behaviors reflected in research showing that almost half of American children between first and third grade want to be thinner and half of nine- to ten-year-old girls are dieting.[2] At least six percent of teens suffer from eating disorders, while many more engage in unhealthy eating behaviors such as fasting, taking diet pills or laxatives, vomiting, and bingeing.[3]

While some use food as a drug to numb their pain, many people turn to actual drugs. As Christians we know better than to use illicit drugs like marijuana, cocaine, or methamphetamines, but you would be surprised to know how many Christians become addicted to prescription medication. The 2013 National Drug Control Strategy Report estimated the number of people abusing prescription drugs at 6.1 million in 2011.[4]

There are three classes of prescription drugs that are most commonly abused:

- Opioids such as codeine, oxycodone, and morphine
- Central nervous system depressants such as barbiturates and benzodiazepines
- Stimulants such as dextroamphetamine and methylphenidate

All of these drugs are legally prescribed by a physician and you may possibly find them in any Christian's medicine cabinet. Yet, according to data from the Substance Abuse and Mental Health Services Administration, the numbers of persons aged twelve or older who received treatment for the use of pain relievers and tranquilizers increased between 2002 and 2011. Numbers of those who received treatment for pain relievers from 2009 to 2011 ranged from 726,000 to 761,000. Sadly, these numbers were greater than the numbers in 2002 to 2005.[5]

Drug addiction is a serious habit to break, and successfully managing an addictive personality usually comes only with the help of a professional or a professional program. In my experience, it seems that some disciples with addiction issues may suffer from untreated depression or bipolar disorder or have other medical and psychological needs that have not been successfully addressed.

Alcohol is not considered a drug by many people, but, when abused, it is just as dangerous as any illicit or legal drug. The fact that it is socially acceptable does not diminish the power that alcohol can hold over a person. According to the National Institute of Alcohol Abuse and Alcoholism (NIAAA), even small amounts of alcohol affect women differently than men. Heavy drinking is always more destructive to women's health than to men's.[6] While some of the whys remain uncertain, the facts from numerous medical studies speak for themselves. An estimated 5.3 million women in the United States drink in a way that threatens their health, safety, and general well-being.[7]

Sadly, alcohol is used by many to numb pain. In 2011, the NIAAA reported that women are at greater risk than men for developing alcohol-related problems and that "heavy drinking increases a woman's risk of becoming a victim of violence and sexual assault."[8]

Unhealthy relationships are another way that people distract themselves from addressing personal issues. In fact, when someone is repeatedly getting involved in unhealthy relationships it can be a sign that there are deeper personal issues. What is an "unhealthy relationship"? The signs of an unhealthy relationship according to The Office on Women's Health (US Department of Health and Human Services) include:

- Focusing all your energy on loving and caring for your partner
- Trying to change your partner to be what you want them to be
- Dropping friends and family or activities you enjoy
- One partner makes all the decisions
- One partner yells, hits, or throws things at the other during arguments
- Having more bad times in the relationship than good[9]

REFLECTION:

How do you typically deal with pain in your life? Are you able to process and manage pain in a healthy way or do you look to activities, things, or people to soothe your pain?

Are there unhealthy patterns, relationships, coping and defense mechanisms, or addictions in your life? Have the methods you have used to change been successful? Have you sought professional support?

In addition to unhealthy methods for dealing with pain, unless we are highly skilled in emotional intelligence, we can put up a wall of defense to keep people out and away from our real problems. These walls are a defense mechanism that we may have built out of self-protection, apathy, and fear. Each brick in these walls has a name or a title:

- Insecurity
- I will never get hurt again or allow someone to hurt me
- Shame
- I will never love or give my heart again
- Fear of rejection
- I will not do anything that I don't feel I could be successful with
- Lack of esteem
- Guilt
- Fear of abandonment

For me, I numbed the pain that resulted from a dysfunctional family and not feeling valued by practically working myself to death. My "tomb" (Matthew 23) was polished with countless acts of service, positions, degrees, acknowledgements, and situations where I was "needed." Unfortunately, much of my striving and achieving was not from totally pure motives. It was not until I was willing to try something different that God's deliverance was granted. In counseling, the effective processing of unresolved painful issues such as grief, shame, insecurity, and fear resulted in heart and soul changes, not just behavioral changes. Professional counseling moved me beyond tireless and repetitive activities that suppressed pain. I learned that the coping mechanisms and anesthetics that worked for me as a child no longer served me well as an adult. We all can choose to face our heart and soul issues, stop doing the same thing over and over again, and leave our "insanity" behind!

REFLECTION:

In what ways have you been doing the same thing over and over again while expecting different results?

Which defense mechanisms (bricks in the wall) have kept you from living God's life to the full (John 10:10) spiritually, emotionally, physically, relationally, or mentally?

Amy's Testimony

From alcoholism and perfectionism...
to healing through safe relationships and professional therapy

In retrospect, the *Healing for Damaged Emotions Workbook* discussion and support group was helpful in awakening my dormant emotions and pinpointing my emotional habits. With the help of professional therapy and guidance from church friends, those old habits are changing. I had pretty much ignored my emotions for a good part of my life.

As a result of growing up with family alcoholics, I still face the challenge of expressing my emotions to my family, and especially to my sister. I have a hard time with my sister as a result of feeling abandoned by her from the time I was eight years old. There was always fighting among my brothers, along with many family secrets and lies. Living in this atmosphere I developed passive-aggressive behaviors.

I am still working on making sure I am not people-pleasing or imprisoned by perfectionism. I am better able to say no when I need to and not feel bad about it. I am also better able to ask for what I need. Having reciprocal relationships is new to me since I didn't have models of two-way relationships as I grew up.

I am excited about learning to enjoy my own company and getting in touch with my tastes and things I like to do. My perfectionism makes me want to procrastinate with going back to school, traveling on my own, and inviting people to spend time with me. The good news is that I have made progress and I don't feel as hurt when friends try to help me grow (reinforcing that I am not perfect), or when they don't have time for me.

God has allowed me to learn not to be so hard on myself when I make mistakes. He has taught me that I am still totally accepted even when I do. When I am having a hard time emotionally, I write my thoughts down, take a prayer walk, sing, and serve others.

Professional therapy has helped me deal with my perfectionism and the dysfunctional characteristics of an adult who grew up with alcoholic parents. The book discussion group provided a safe place for me to explore, share, and feel acceptance.

Chapter Eight

Our Fathers

Fathers, do not exasperate your children; instead, bring them
up in the training and instruction of the Lord (Ephesians 6:4).

The righteous lead blameless lives;
blessed are their children after them (Proverbs 20:7).

I'm sure that you've heard that our parents have tremendous influence in every area of our lives. I remember seeing one comedic sketch that showed a couple in their own bed with both sets of their parents subconsciously speaking in their ears. There is no shortage of research testifying to the impact our fathers have on our lives. Let's take a look at a few of the statistics.

Researchers at Columbia University found that teens living in two-parent households who have a poor relationship with their father are 68 percent more likely to smoke, drink, or use drugs compared to all teens in two-parent households. Teens in single-mother households don't fare well either. They had a 30 percent higher risk for drug and alcohol abuse than those in all two-parent households.[1]

The US Department of Health found that 63 percent of teen suicides come from fatherless homes.[2] That's five times the national average. *Justice and Behavior* reports that 90 percent of all runaways and homeless children are from fatherless homes. That's 32 times the national average. They also found that 80 percent of rapists with anger problems come from fatherless homes. That's 14 times the national average.[3] The Centers for Disease Control discovered that 85 percent of children with behavioral problems come from fatherless homes. That's 20 times the national average.[4]

A National Principals Association Report states that 71 percent of all high school dropouts come from fatherless homes. That's nine times the national average.[5] Rainbows for All God's Children discovered that 75 percent of all adolescent patients in chemical abuse centers come from fatherless homes. That's ten times the national average.[6] The US Department of Justice reports that 85 percent of all youths in prison come from fatherless homes. That's 20 times the national average.[7]

Daughters of single parents without a father involved are 53 percent more likely to marry as teenagers, 711 percent more likely to have children as teenagers, 164 percent more likely to have a premarital birth, and 92 percent more likely to get divorced themselves.[8]

Jennifer Roback Morse of the Hoover Institution writes, "Without two parents, working together as a team, the child has more difficulty learning the combination of empathy, reciprocity, fairness and self-command that people ordinarily take for granted. If the child does not learn this at home, society will have to manage his behavior in some other way. He may have to be rehabilitated, incarcerated, or otherwise restrained. In this case, prisons will substitute for parents."[9]

You have probably heard that our relationships with our fathers profoundly impact our relationship with God. I have heard that because of difficult relationships with their own fathers, some people even struggle with prayers that are addressed to God as our Father. It is sometimes difficult for them to separate their earthly father from our Father God. There is probably some post-traumatic stress involved, yet these disciples show us that our physical fathers do make a deep mark on our lives.

My Dad

On Saturday, August 22, 2009 I drove from New Jersey down to Washington DC to take my father to the Prince George's County Hospital. He had problems walking and thought that maybe it was sciatica. The doctors were kind and also believed that my dad had a problem with a sciatic nerve. I took him back home to the house he built with his own hands, made sure his needs were met and headed home to New Jersey.

Unknown to me, Dad spent the following days in bed, in pain and unable to move, eat, or do much of anything. Once I became aware of it, I struggled about what I should do from my home in New Jersey. My dad was always a calculating man who had a plan for everything. He had set up an appointment with his primary care physician for that Friday. In a subsequent call, he mentioned that he thought he may have had a heart attack. Some of his favorite words were, "You big dummy butt," and that's all I could think of him as he resisted going to the hospital that day. After consultation with a number of people, I called the ambulance myself. I struggled with this decision, because I wasn't sure if the call would be helpful or harmful. No one could ever make my dad, "Smickey" Jones, do anything he didn't want to do! The last thing I wanted was for my dad to be angry with me. Well, actually, the last thing I wanted was not to have my dad! So, I made the call.

As I figured, he was angry with me, refused to go to the hospital with the ambulance, lectured me on how he had to plan everything, and gave me all of his reasons why he had planned the doctor's visit on Friday. Though he was in excruciating pain, he felt he needed to make sure that he had showered and changed his clothes since he had not been able to do so the entire week.

I can't remember all of the details, but somehow, Dad ended up in the Washington DC Veterans Hospital. I went back down to DC to see him that Saturday, August 29. The VA attempted a surgery to clear a blockage between his intestines and liver. This was unsuccessful and I drove down the following weekend to transport my dad to George Washington Hospital where another team of experts would try to clear up the blockage. After two decades as a disciple under constant pressure from my dad to get married, he quickly gave my friend who accompanied me his permission to marry me. Hilarious was the only word that came to mind.

Since Dad was always an exemplary planner and a miser, he had thought through plans for his money. He knew that if anything happened to him, since his mother was the beneficiary of his bonds, the money would really be "thrown away" to the Maryland system where my 101-year-old grandmother was in a nursing home. Shockingly, Smickey Jones allowed me to come down to DC and cash out all of his bonds, just in case anything happened. I took two days off from my new job and went to DC on Tuesday, September 15. Dad was always a jokester, so when the George Washington Hospital patient advocate confirmed that he knew what he was doing in signing the power of attorney, he said, "Yeah, I'm giving away all my money." Though I expected everything to be okay with my dad, I also inherited his nature of planning. We both typically would rather be safe than sorry.

We spoke about his progress that day and the next and planned for his move to a rehabilitation facility so that he could regain his strength and go back home. For some reason, during this visit, my dad mentioned that he had cancer. I knew he was feeling depressed about being in the hospital so long, but this was crazy! I immediately became an emotional basket case. I believe that God sent a hospital chaplain by that day to help me think through my dad's statement. The announcement was a devastating shock to me, so I asked the doctors about this. The lead doctor said that my dad did not have cancer. I rejoiced, got myself somewhat together and headed home. I was back at work on Thursday and Friday.

On Monday evening, September 21, I called my father as I had been doing pretty much every day. He wasn't the same Smickey Jones I had been dealing with for forty-two years. He actually asked me if he could give my phone number to a gentleman in the hospital whom he had seen take care of everyone on the floor including the doctors and nurses. My father had previously spewed out many hurtful and embarrassing words about my beloved single status but never really seemed to proactively support moving me to Mrs. I was encouraged that he was not badgering me about having grandchildren (for him) and that he was actually showing empathy and active care.

On top of that, the typically emotionally distant, nonvulnerable and nonexpressive Vernon Jones said that he was "afraid that I wasn't going to call him that night." I assured him that he was "my honey" and that "of course I was going to call." I was really shocked with his expression of desire for connection. I don't remember my dad ever being that vulnerable. Though I started telling my dad that I loved him all the more when I became a Christian, he wouldn't or couldn't verbally express the same. We talked for a bit more about how he was doing, how the extreme swelling was in his legs, and plans to move him to a rehabilitation facility as soon as the paperwork was completed. We both felt frustrated with the slowness of that process.

At work, while sitting at my desk on Tuesday morning, September 22, I got the call from the hospital. Finally, I thought, they have the paperwork complete for Dad to move to a rehabilitation center. I had done the research, made calls, talked to his neighbors, and had options for the move. It had been an entire month since I first took dad to the Prince George's County Hospital. I thought, if the George Washington doctors couldn't fix the extreme swelling and get it down, who could? But the doctor on the other end of the phone line had not called to tell me that my father was ready to make the move to the rehabilitation facility.

The doctor told me that they had found my father "unresponsive." Maybe I said, "OK…" with a big question mark, not sure what that meant. He then explained that someone went into my dad's room and that my dad did not respond. My dad was no longer breathing. My dad had passed. I sat at my desk not really believing what I had heard. I was stunned, shocked, paralyzed, dumbfounded, completely numb. I couldn't move. I really couldn't think. My coworker and secretary had to tell me that I needed to go home. It was all so surreal!

The grief that I felt was very complicated. Though I loved my dad as no one else, our relationship had always been complex and challenging. The more I read about and studied psychology and had my own counseling sessions, the more I understood how narcissistically injured, depressed, and troubled my dad was. After hearing about how he grew up and how he served in the army and then as a DC police officer in the 1960s, I grew to feel even more sympathy for my dad and his isolated life.

My Stepfather

Though I have considered my life to be blessed by God and in his hands, the separation and divorce of my parents had a profound impact on me. I really did not consider the extent of the impact until my adult life when I was fortunate enough to receive professional counseling. After Mom decided to leave Dad in 1974, we moved from Washington DC to Landover, Maryland. My sister and I joked that we'd moved into Beverly Hills as opposed to the Bradley Hills apartment complex. Mom seemed to be well pursued, as I remember a number of boyfriends before she became serious about her future husband. They had grown up in the same Philadelphia neighborhood and reconnected in 1977 after we moved to Philadelphia from Maryland. Mom had a freak accident and injured the nerves in her hand. She could no longer continue the work she was doing in an office and soon thereafter, this man moved into our home. We were supposed to be a "family," but from the beginning I didn't like him. Most children would rather have their parents stay together, and I also felt that he tried to "buy us" with activities and goodies. At ten years old, I was not trying to accept a new father.

I don't remember many of the details, but it became obvious that my stepfather had a drinking problem. Along with the chaos that living with an alcoholic wreaks on a home, much anxiety came with this addiction.

I always felt that I had to walk around on egg shells to make sure that my stepfather was happy, that there could be nothing around the house to anger him. Despite Mom riding us to keep everything in order, I remember my stepfather fussing all the time. As a result of his instability, our financial problems escalated and we moved from Philadelphia to Greensboro, North Carolina. I personally was happy that we moved because there really didn't seem to be much of anything positive going on in North Philadelphia.

Sadly, it seems that the number of children who grow up in homes where the adults have some type of addiction problem keeps increasing. With my stepfather, there always seemed to be drama, problems paying bills, anger, blaming, scapegoating, and very little talk about the "elephant in the middle of the room," the core of the problems. My brother seemed to become the comedian, and as I shared previously, I tried to make myself invisible while my brother and sister were the scapegoats diverting much of the attention. My study of roles in a dysfunctional family helped me to see how I became codependent by nature from the time that we took the responsibility for my stepfather's happiness.

Though there was great rejoicing when my mom, sister, brother, and stepfather all studied the Bible and were baptized into Christ, salvation in no way equals sanctification. We are completely in error if we believe that the "new creation" we become in Christ all of a sudden eliminates the challenges, deficiencies of character, and strongholds that Satan has embedded in our lives, hearts, minds, and souls.

The more I talk to people about growing up in a dysfunctional home, the more I find that most of us did. I have heard many jokingly ask if anyone even knows what a "functional" home or family looks like.

REFLECTION:

What positive and negative impact has your father had on you and your family?

The Impact of a Father

There is no denying that our fathers or the significant men in our childhoods have a major impact on our lives. In *What a Difference a Daddy Makes: The Indelible Imprint a Dad Leaves on His Daughter's Life,* Dr. Kevin Leman asserts, "You tell me if a woman chooses Dennis Rodman over Michael Jordan, and I'll give you an accurate picture of her father!"[10] Because fathers strongly impact their children, many psychologists will tell us that, what a father does will be repeated in a woman's relationships with men over and over. How we view our father impacts who we will marry and our view of ourselves and of God. It is very important that we comprehensively understand how our family of origin has made us who we are today—spiritually, emotionally, socially, and mentally. Who we are has been shaped by all of the significant people in our lives. Our parents continue to influence us today in our relationships with God, ourselves, and others. We must understand this influence.

Even without horror stories of neglect and abuse, it is sometimes very difficult for people to uncover pain, disappointments, failed relationships, and wounds from our parents. This work takes facing our truths bravely! Time alone does not heal all wounds. I'm sure you've seen many people who have allowed their hurt and pain to fester and destroy their lives and relationships.

REFLECTION:

How has your family of origin made you who you are today emotionally and relationally? How is your character like those of your parents?

_____

_____

_____

As a result of my childhood, one of the areas I have extensively researched, examined, and discussed is that of adult children of alcoholics. I feel blessed to have had the opportunity to spend a number of evenings with some of them in Adult Children of Alcoholics (ACOA), a 12-step group like Alcoholics Anonymous. The group members shared their experiences, challenges, victories, and desire to grow. In confidence, we supported each other and learned together through the reading and discussing of a few books. At that time, resources that helped me the most in this area of personal growth were those provided by Dr. Janet G. Woititz. She has written a number of books and is probably most known for her articulation of the characteristics of adult children of alcoholics. When I first read her description, most of the traits described who I am by nature. She shared that "as long as things are going smoothly, ACOAs are fine. However, when they experience conflict, controversy, or crises they respond with less-than-adult-like reactions."[11] Typical traits of adult children of alcoholics or adult children of dysfunctional families can be found through any Internet search engine.

One of the most insightful books I read in my efforts to understand the impact of my dad and stepfather was *A Dad-Shaped Hole in My Heart: How God Wants to Heal the Wounds Left by Your Earthly Father.* H. Norman Wright asserts that "there are many daughters walking around with a hole in their heart in the shape of their father. They are missing something from their father that should have been given."[12] Unconsciously, we can attempt to fill this dad-shaped hole through other means although we fail over and over again. Though I could share many resources about the major areas I have worked through, the question for each of us is how much work have we done personally? Have you thoroughly evaluated the impact your family of origin and your father have had on your life—whether he was present or not?

Since our families have such a deep and lasting impact on us, it is extremely important that we understand family dynamics. Please consider the following questions, research the topics, and journal your thoughts and feelings:

- How would you describe your relationship with your father, mother, and siblings?

- In what ways were your parents there for you? In what ways were your parents not there for you?

- What have you done to attempt to fill the void that exists if your father or mother was absent or the relationship lacking? Have these strategies been successful?

- How has your relationship with your father affected your relationship with Jesus and God?

- Do you know the four parenting styles human development researchers have categorized, along with their impact?

- If your parents were divorced, do you know the common characteristics of adult children of divorce?

- What is the possible impact of an emotionally or physically absent father or mother?

- What is the predictable impact of verbally or emotionally abusive parents?

- What is the typical impact of sexually abusive parents or other family members?

- Have you been able to forgive and wish well any significant men or women who have harmed you or did not have your best interests in mind?

- What unfinished business needs to be addressed in your relationship with your parents?

- What do you wish was true about your personal and family history? Do you have losses that need to be felt and effectively grieved?

At various times, my father and stepfather could be described as emotionally unavailable, depressed, funny, intelligent, explosive, angry, sad, very guarded, cynical, over-responsible, not responsible, alcoholic, one who objectified women, unresponsive to needs, developmentally challenged, and unpredictable. I have learned that as a result, fears of abandonment and rejection are ingrained in my heart and soul. I feel that I have worked most of my life to prove my value and to "gain permission" to take up space here on earth. This prison of unworthiness and Satan's strongholds are being destroyed block by block with each effort I have made to focus on healing and growing in my character—heart and soul. God has given me the courage to process the grief and losses I attempted to ignore.

I appreciate Wright's admonition that "grief is the road to recovery. It enables you to move on with your life." A number of disciples have mistakenly attempted to leave the past behind at their baptism. Wright also states, "Forgetting is not the key to forgiveness. Remembering is,"[13] and "What is forgotten is unavailable and what is unavailable cannot be healed."[14] Paul does encourage us to forget what is behind and press on (Philippians 3:13–14), but "to forget past pain, we need to make peace with our past."[15] Forgiveness and grieving losses are more than just simple decisions. They are both processes. **Only once we have successfully and effectively grieved our losses can we leave them behind.**

H. Norman Wright also describes common heart problems in daughters as the bruised heart, the performance heart, the hardened heart, and the addicted heart. I could totally relate to all of the heart problems Wright discusses. At different times, I personally have felt beaten down, not good enough, too much, inadequate, ashamed, fearful, insecure, and in need of attention, approval, support, and validation. Many times, I lived in survival mode and at other times I strove to be the perfect daughter, student, friend, or whatever was needed so that I would not be considered a failure or disappointment. Though I didn't know it, through activities, goals, accomplishments, perfectionism, and even work in the church, I was obsessively and compulsively striving to cover the pain that I had not faced. I remember someone saying that I occasionally seemed like an "angry black man" in some ways. Unfortunately, since it doesn't work, perfectionism is typically accompanied by guilt and anger. Like many abandoned daughters, I have also probably searched for a substitute for my father where this neglect is repeated. Throughout my life, I had suppressed my emotions and thus, as Shrek was told by Donkey, had many onion layers that needed to be peeled away. I think I mentioned that I love animated films!

Wright also shares that, "A girl abandoned by the first man in her life feels tossed aside, unworthy or incapable of receiving a man's love."[16] When fathers haven't been there for their daughters, the result has been labeled "Fatherless Daughter Syndrome." Wright kindly provides symptoms of this syndrome.

Many fatherless children grapple with fears of rejection, abandonment, and commitment. Some struggle with sexuality, overfunctioning, and overachieveing. Unfortunately, many have been found to have anger and depression issues. Unless these issues are dealt with at the core (heart and soul) and the grief of this ambiguous loss is effectively processed, these symptoms can lead to emotional, social, and even spiritual demise. The same can be said of children who have been adopted or who have lost their fathers at an early age. It is imperative that we face and effectively process all of the emotions and compulsions that stem from being fatherless children.

I take time to mention these symptoms because I frequently hear from discouraged disciples who have received assistance that has only touched the edges of their symptoms. Unless someone is a licensed psychologist, therapist, or social worker, they probably do not have the skills needed to deal with complicated issues below the surface of symptoms and outward behaviors. I sincerely appreciate church leaders who understand when disciples' issues need attention beyond their capability. It is insanity when we continually attempt the same ineffective tactics over and over again, tactics that lead to frustrated, disheartened, and disillusioned Christians giving up on their relationship with God and efforts to live a righteous life.

REFLECTION:

Can you relate to any of my experiences? Are there any issues or feelings about your father that you need to more effectively process?

_____

_____

_____

Since becoming a disciple in 1986, and especially since beginning professional counseling in 2003, I worked hard to improve my relationship with my father. I developed better boundaries, gained the courage to call my father out on his inappropriate comments, planned a counseling session that included him, asked for what I wanted and needed, and asked him to change. I pushed through his resistance and was able to accept the areas where my dad would not change. It was so important that I grew to the point of giving up the dream of my father being what I wanted and needed him to be. I had previously and incessantly desired and fought to get "water from a rock." Breakthroughs were celebrated as I was able to give my father "permission" to be who he was and also give myself the right to protect myself from my dad's unhealthy behaviors. Getting to this point and level of emotional maturity also included the process of forgiving myself for not being self-sufficient, for having needs, for not being perfect, and for failing to be important enough to the most important people around me for them to change. I had to accept what I thought was unacceptable to others.

As you can probably imagine, since God's intention was for us to grow up with two godly parents, the positive impact of fathers has been lauded in scientific research. Though many of us grew up in less than optimal, if not highly dysfunctional situations, there are, of course, many examples of wonderful husbands and fathers. Imagine if you will the opposite of the statistics at the beginning of the chapter. I won't bore you with all the detailed statistics that can quickly be accessed, but children with involved fathers have been found to be more confident, better able to deal with frustration, better able to gain independence and their own identity, more likely to mature into compassionate adults, more likely to have a high self-esteem, more sociable, more secure as infants, less likely to show signs of depression, less likely to commit suicide, and more empathetic. Boys with involved fathers have been shown to be less aggressive and adolescent girls are less likely to engage in sex.

Fathers and Sons

Many times, men who have grown up with their fathers can be just as emotionally damaged and confused as men who have been abandoned by their fathers. Boys learn how to be a man and a husband through the modeling of their father. During a Father's Day speech, President Barack Obama stated, "I know the toll it took on me, not having a father in the house; the hole in your heart when you don't have a male figure in the home who can guide you and lead you. So I resolved many years ago that it was my obligation to break the cycle—that, if I could be anything in life, I would be a good father to my children."[17] Just as with daughters, sons with absent fathers, like President Obama, can be very successful in some areas. In fact, if a father was not present to provide approval, men abandoned by their fathers often seek success to fill the hole in their hearts.

You may have heard that the most important influence a father has on his child is through his relationship with the mother. This father-and-mother relationship teaches boys how to treat girls and girls how they should be treated by boys. What a different world we would have if men were able to fulfill God's plan for their lives and families.

Abandonment Recovery

One bit of good news is that abandonment issues and all the accompanying feelings can be managed. Of course you have heard that an alcoholic cannot begin recovery without first admitting that they are an alcoholic. The same applies for adults who were abandoned by a parent. In brief, adults who were abandoned by a parent can sometimes feel the following:

- A big hole in your heart or an emptiness that cannot be filled
- Sad when you see positive interactions between parents and their children
- Low self-esteem and feelings of worthlessness
- Angry at the world (for no known reason)
- Unsafe, anxious, and on edge
- Fear of abandonment and rejection in relationships
- That there is something wrong with you
- Emotionally dependent on the opposite sex and resentful of them for it
- Distrust of the opposite sex or idealization of them
- Invisible or not heard
- Chronically in need of approval of others
- The need to be perfect at any cost
- Conflicting feeling towards God

REFLECTION:

If one or both of your parents were emotionally or physically absent, have you recognized and effectively processed any of the above feelings?

Again, more prayer, fasting, and Bible study alone will not likely heal the deep impact of abandonment or an unhealthy relationship with a parent on one's self-esteem and interpersonal relationships. Sometimes we need help from a professional counselor so that paradigms (negative tapes) can be reprogramed and the relationships renegotiated. While attempting to deal with abandonment issues without a strong spiritual foundation will be immensely frustrating, families of origin have such a deep impact that professional counseling is often the most effective and efficient way to attack the issues that come with deep-seated dysfunction. In private time and counseling sessions, the following activities helped me and can be helpful in your healing journey:

- Pray for an improved relationship with your parent(s).

- Pray for an emotional attachment to develop with your parent(s).

- Work to get in touch with and express your emotions.

- Work to fight against idealizing an absent parent(s).

- Plan to improve your relationship (meet and spend time) with your parent(s).

- Deal with the anger that is displayed in efforts to be the exact opposite of the absent parent(s).

- Discuss the abandonment impact on your self-esteem since many children believe that they deserved to be abandoned or that they were a burden to the parent.

- Read books about what you struggle with.

- Have a joint session with the parent(s) and a counselor.

Our Father God

The best news of all is that we can each have a special relationship with God. We have a Heavenly Father who always protects us, provides for us, cares for us, and loves us! It's good to know that we are created in God's image and not the reverse. He is not like some of our fathers who have not lived up to his calling. Amen that God's ways are higher and holier than ours.

It has sometimes been difficult for me to separate how the significant men in my life have treated me from the desires and love our Father God has for me. Though I have had little difficulty intellectually understanding God's love letter (the Bible), it has been exponentially more difficult to internalize his love for me in my heart and soul. For those who have searched hard and long for a father or for our own absent or emotionally unavailable fathers, knowing that God has created us to be with him and that he is waiting for us in heaven can provide the peace that transcends all understanding (Philippians 4:7). I am so very grateful that the resources I have accessed have helped me to understand that God does not expect me to be perfect. I have had to work extremely hard and process much grief to get to the point where I am better able to see myself as God sees me. My hope and prayer is that your personal work can lead you to this understanding as Paul prayed in Ephesians 3:16–19:

> I pray that out of his glorious riches he may strengthen you with power through his Spirit in your inner being, so that Christ may dwell in your *hearts* through faith. And I pray that you, being rooted and established in love, may have power, together with all the Lord's holy people, to grasp how wide and long and high and deep is the love of Christ, and to know this love that surpasses knowledge—that you may be filled to the measure of all the fullness of God (emphasis added).

REFLECTION:

Have you been able to clear out enough emotional sewage so that you can internalize God's wide, long, high, and deep love for you?

Related Scriptures for Personal Study

It's encouraging to know that despite any issue, struggle, or trauma, we can be transformed and renewed in the spirit of our minds, and that our paradigms can change!

Do not conform to the pattern of this world, but be transformed by the renewing of your mind. Then you will be able to test and approve what God's will is—his good, pleasing and perfect will (Romans 12:2).

Finally, brothers and sisters, whatever is true, whatever is noble, whatever is right, whatever is pure, whatever is lovely, whatever is admirable—if anything is excellent or praiseworthy—think about such things (Philippians 4:8).

You were taught, with regard to your former way of life, to put off your old self, which is being corrupted by its deceitful desires (Ephesians 4:22).

Though my father and mother forsake me,
    the LORD will receive me (Psalm 27:10).

"Never will I leave you;
    never will I forsake you" (Hebrews 13:5).

But may the righteous be glad
    and rejoice before God;
    may they be happy and joyful (Psalm 68:3).

It is for freedom that Christ has set us free. Stand firm, then, and do not let yourselves be burdened again by a yoke of slavery (Galatians 5:1).

The LORD is close to the brokenhearted
and saves those who are crushed in spirit (Psalm 34:18).

See to it that no one falls short of the grace of God and that no bitter root grows up to cause trouble and defile many (Hebrews 12:15).

Camila's Testimony

From shut down by multigenerational dysfunctions...
to healing through God's love and forgiving myself

The *Healing for Damaged Emotions Workbook* helped me more once I finished it as opposed to when I first read and discussed the chapters. At the time of the discussions, because of my emotions, my heart and mind were not open because of a number of disappointments. I experienced a lot of challenges in my childhood and even as an adult. What keeps me in bondage more than anything are my relationships with the family members I would like to be closer to (my parents, sisters, brothers, and children). Since my parents did not understand the meaning of love (1 Corinthians 13) nor of healthy relationships, our dysfunctional behaviors have been passed down from generation to generation.

What has changed the most for me is my willingness to finally say that I really had not forgiven anyone. Though I made a decision to forgive, I wasn't able to do so in my heart. Satan had me think that I had forgiven those who had harmed me. Since I had not even been able to forgive myself, my resentments, frustrations, and bitterness were still deeply rooted in my heart, mind, and soul. I wasn't able to truly accept God's grace for me, didn't give grace to myself, and thus was not capable of giving grace to others. Though dealing with all of these issues and doing all I can to mature emotionally has been really hard, I am grateful for 2 Peter 3:8–9:

> But do not forget this one thing, dear friends: With the Lord a day is like a thousand years, and a thousand years are like a day. The Lord is not slow in keeping his promise, as some understand slowness. Instead he is patient with you, not wanting anyone to perish, but everyone to come to repentance.

I feel that God was patiently waiting for me to get to the point where I can "let go and let God" by taking my emotions and hurts to the cross. I see that I was collecting debts by holding onto my harmful emotions and records of wrong.

Though my parents did the best they knew how, from age eighteen until age thirty-nine, I was on drugs and smoked cigarettes. Because of God's grace and mercy, I am learning to love him more, to love myself, and to forgive myself. I am so grateful that God has allowed me to restart my spiritual journey through his salvation and my recovery process through a 12-step program. Though I am HIV positive, I now can accept that I am made in his image, and I take up my armor (Ephesians 6:10–17) to fight Satan's attacks on a daily basis.

Chapter Nine

How to Change:
More than Just a Decision

We are products of our past, but we don't have to be prisoners of it. —Rick Warren

Be diligent in these matters; give yourself wholly to them, so that everyone may see your progress (1 Timothy 4:15).

The Process Takes Time

We live in a microwave society. It seems that even the fast-food restaurants are not fast enough for some of us. In order to keep our attention, our television shows change scenes at least every thirty seconds. We want everything and we want it now. But one thing that we need to clearly understand is that **change, repentance, healing, and forgiveness are all processes.** We have rightfully learned that these processes begin with decisions. Yet, the reality is that it takes time and an effective process for many of these decisions to change us from the inside out and to help us to forgive where we need to.

This is a problem for me. As I've told you, I am an achiever. I typically like to work on something and get it done as quickly as possible. I've had to let myself off the hook and remember that it didn't take a week to develop my sinful characteristics, dysfunctional thinking, and self-sabotaging behaviors, and it surely will take more than a week to substantially change them. Also, in my typically (definitely not always) logical thinking, I'd rather try to do something right and as efficiently as possible the first time as opposed to working hard at throwing dull darts at a target that continues to move. In the business world, there is often talk about working smarter and not just harder. These thoughts have helped me in my efforts to change at a heart and soul level rather than just changing my behavior.

REFLECTION:

In what areas have you been seeking a quick-fix route to change rather than patiently focusing on making every effort to become more like Jesus on a heart and soul level? What adjustments do you need to make to have lasting change, repentance, or forgiveness?

_____

_____

_____

Describe the character-change process as you know it.

_____

_____

_____

In education, business, life coaching, counseling, and social work, we learn about the change process. There's a pretty interesting game called Making Change Happen[1] that education experts use with school districts as they begin thinking through a change process. Yet, as I have noted in over twenty years as a disciple, it seems that we are just recently beginning to formally discuss the change process. Disciples have published great books (such as *Repentance, Mind Change, and Deep Convictions*) and we hear a lot of sermons about the need to change, how we need to be more like Jesus, and what we specifically need to change, but we need more regarding how to achieve that change. This lack of specific direction and knowledge has frustrated many Christians and has left many folks spinning wheels in their quiet times and Christian walk. Unless we understand why we behave as we do and seek to heal the pain that leads to dysfunction, we'll continue to spin our wheels. I am very encouraged by the disciples' desire to change and to be pleasing to our amazing God, but we need to do a better job equipping each other to understand the change and growth process.

How many disciples do you know who have struggles with or have been beaten by the same temptation or character flaw year after year, fast after fast, prayer after prayer, conference after conference, and discipling time after discipling time? For example, one brother shared with me that he knew of only one single brother (now married) who did not give in to masturbation. I was surprised and very saddened. As you know, none of our issues are likely to simply disappear without properly addressing them from the heart. I am so proud of and encouraged by the Central New Jersey Church of Christ brothers (married and single) and brothers like them in other congregations who meet on a weekly basis to help each other overcome struggles and addictions.

Of course I don't discount Paul's message regarding how God provides his perfect power in our weakness (2 Corinthians 12:9), yet Paul also told us to let everyone see our progress: "Be diligent in these matters; give yourself wholly to them, so that everyone may see your progress" (1 Timothy 4:15). We all need to continually consider what true, heart and soul character progress we have made from the inside out. I have noticed that it is too easy and too common for people to "paste on discipleship" and "white-knuckle" our way through. God's plan is that we become a new creation (2 Corinthians 5:17) and continuously progress in our sanctification.

REFLECTION:

Have you been plagued by the same struggles and sins throughout your discipleship, despite your Christian regimen? If so, what are they? Why do you think there has not been lasting change?

Whole-Person and Systematic Approaches to Change

We know that we can't ride a bike if a tire is ruined because one or more of the spokes have been broken. For some reason, too many of us seem to think that we can just focus on our spiritual health without regard to our emotional, physical, mental, financial, professional, and relational health. All of these components of our being are intrinsically connected. We can't be like Jesus, who did everything well (Mark 7:37), if we just focus on one of these areas while ignoring the others. Lack of self-control or discipline in one area will rear its ugly head in other areas unless we address the underlying character issues, heart and soul.

We are well aware of the fact that, in order to help athletes consistently perform at optimal levels, sports coaches address not only the physical aspect of their players, but also the mental and emotional factors. Many top athletes hire sports psychologists in their efforts to overcome "stinking thinking" that gets in the way of achieving their goals. Most school teachers, oncologists, parents, mentors, life coaches, and others responsible for progress and growth efforts know they must consider not just physical, IQ, or personality factors, but also the emotional part of our being.

Our desire for quick fixes and results-oriented discipleship has led many to madly attempt behavior changes without knowing how to change hearts and souls. Granted, most of us are doing our absolute best to be like Jesus and to help others to be like him too. What's sometimes missing is knowledge of how to change ourselves and others from the inside out. This lack of knowledge isn't anyone's "fault" per se. Yet, we do call it insanity when we continue to use the same methods and expect different results. Once we know better we can do and be better! 2 Peter 1:5 calls us to add to our faith knowledge. If we want authentic growth and change, we have to take our knowledge higher and deeper.

Certified professional life coaches who are trained to help others reach their goals typically take at least sixteen hours of classes, take assessments, conduct practice sessions, and use scientific tools. Licensed mental health counselors or social workers are charged with an interdisciplinary, multifaceted, holistic process of promoting healthy lifestyles, identifying levels of functioning and roadblocks, and optimizing mental health. These professionals typically take sixty college credit hours and at least nineteen courses, engage in 1,000 hours of practicum and internship, practice for two years under a supervisor, and *then* take a state licensing exam. To summarize their practices and the vast array of books that discuss the change process in one chapter is impossible. I hope that this chapter will be a springboard for our efforts to get to the heart and soul love God desires for us.

Process for Lifetrap Changes

Many authors, psychologists, researchers, and Christian leaders have delineated processes for change. We all want to know how we can be transformed on a heart and soul level. In Young and Klosko's *Reinventing Your Life: The Breakthrough Program to End Negative Behavior...and Feel Great Again,* the authors provide steps for lifetrap changes. They describe lifetraps as long-term patterns that are deeply ingrained and hard to change. These include unhealthy thinking that keeps us trapped in certain areas of our lives. The authors aptly note that change in these areas usually requires the willingness to endure the pain that comes with it. Their recommended steps for changing lifetraps are as follows:

- Label and identify your lifetraps.
- Understand the childhood origins of your lifetrap. Feel the wounded child inside you.
- Build a case against your lifetrap. Disprove its validity at a rational level.
- Write letters to the parent, sibling, or peer who helped cause your lifetrap.
- Examine your lifetrap pattern in careful detail.
- Work on pattern-breaking.
- Forgive your parents.[2]

Young and Klosko expertly expound upon all eight of the steps for lifetrap changes and share examples of clients who work through the process. They also provide a questionnaire so that readers can determine which of eleven lifetraps are most pertinent to their lives. The eleven articulated lifetraps relate to a lack of security or safety, one's ability to function independently, one's strength of emotional connections to others, self-esteem, self-expression, and one's ability to accept realistic limits. For the most effective and efficient change process, working through these steps with a licensed counselor is recommended.

REFLECTION:

Which, if any, of the lifetraps categories above, articulated by Young and Klosko, are issues in your life?

_____

_____

_____

Have you ever attacked a character challenge or negative behavior using this type of process?

_____

_____

_____

To which personal-change goals (overcoming recurring sins; raising your level of emotional intelligence; defeating lifetraps, strongholds, and struggles) can you apply this process?

_____

_____

_____

It is also helpful that Young and Klosko discuss common obstacles to change. Being aware of emotional, spiritual, and social paradigms and behaviors that can derail our efforts to change will improve our prospects for personal growth and transformation. What's wonderful about *Reinventing Your Life* is that the authors also discuss steps for dealing with their eight common obstacles. They are able to provide this information as a result of years of school, training, and professional counseling. Though the heart and soul growth process will not be exactly the same for any two people, general principles provided by professionals like these are usually very helpful to most.

REFLECTION:

Are you aware of any obstacles that have impeded your efforts to change?

Of course, broad-based and targeted Bible study, helpful books, discipling times, prayer times, fasting, and making every effort can lead to change. Yet, I really am baffled by the entrenched negative attitudes of some towards professional counseling as another vital tool for change. If we limit our self-care and growth potential only to our spiritual dimension we neglect our mental, emotional, and even physical dimensions. I know a brother, who is held in regard, who *only* uses the Bible to try to change his character. At the time of our conversations, he had never read a Christian-authored book for growth. I'm sure you may have heard people say that "the Bible can fix everything," but in fact it is God who can fix everything, and to do this he has provided us with many types of resources in addition to his word. Some believe that there is no need for disciples to take medicine or consult with a professional counselor (psychologist) or life coach. I honestly can only think that this brother's resistance is the reason why he continues to be socially inept, along with being controlled and imprisoned by insecurities and the devastating impact of past traumas and sins. I am eternally grateful that many spiritual leaders and disciples recognize and have been humble enough to admit that the training most of us have received is not sufficient for effectively counseling disciples through the process of changing their lifetraps.

I am also bewildered by the fact that most of us have little problem consulting an oncologist when we are threatened with cancer; a cardiologist when our heart is failing; a specialist supported by a team of additional medical specialists once diagnosed with HIV/AIDs; or finding the absolute best doctor available, even if they are located in a different country, when one of our children is on their deathbed; but we have an aversion to the specialists that have been trained to help us with heart and soul issues and our emotional and mental health. I understand that many have fears when it comes to these types of "private" and even stigmatized struggles. I sincerely believe that working on these areas takes the faith and courage we tapped into when we decided to become disciples. I have frequently termed my personal growth process as "being born again emotionally." During it, I have experienced many of the feelings, responses, fears, challenges, and victories that accompanied being born again spiritually. Unfortunately, this includes persecution. Those who do not have knowledge about emotional intelligence and mental health issues are sometimes afraid of these topics, and some have chosen to shun, dismiss, or persecute those who desire to follow a whole-person approach to their relationship with God as opposed to having the courage to research and even work on the areas that need attention in their own lives. Indeed, there are Christian counselors and life coaches available in most places if one prefers an integrated rather than a purely clinical approach. In my worldwide church fellowship, Christian counseling is now even available online (http://dtcounselorconnect.com/). Appendix II includes information on when to see a professional counselor, psychologist, or psychiatrist.

No matter the preference, we have to ask ourselves if we're willing to do whatever it takes to "get well" (John 5:6) and be all that God has called us to be. We also need to increase our knowledge in these areas so that we will not further burden those who have emotional or mental health challenges (Matthew 18:6).

REFLECTION:

Why do you think that shame is sometimes attached to mental or emotional health issues and professional counseling assistance? Why would we see a psychologist or psychiatrist differently than an oncologist, podiatrist, cardiologist, or ophthalmologist? How are these viewed among your family, community, and congregation?

The Power of Great Questions

In my life coach training and practice along with the training I received as an educator and school administrator, I learned that effective questioning is imperative. Through my own personal counseling sessions, powerful (even if simple) questions have made all the difference in my growth. Many of you are familiar with the statement made famous by Stephen Covey, "Seek first to understand." We will make so much more sustained progress if we shift from a focus on the effort to label behaviors (prideful, selfish, lazy, and so on) to a focus on **understanding why we behave and think the way we do.** Such understanding is necessary for any true change. I have found that we usually don't get to the root or core of any issue until we have asked "Why?" a number of times. This takes the patience that is the first characteristic of love listed in 1 Corinthians 13. It takes no work and no love to shamefully call someone prideful or selfish. Typically folks who frequently throw these words out simply don't know what else to do.

I wish I could share the sixteen hours of training I received for life coaching. I call it discipling with a systematic and research-based process. Since I can't share everything, I will share some of the most important questions we need to ask ourselves and others as we seek to articulate and reach our character, relational, spiritual, emotional, professional, financial, and health goals.

For each goal we articulate, the following questions can help to develop the understanding and motivation necessary for success:

- What will achieving your goal mean to you? Specifically, how will you feel? What will this look like in your life? What would you hear once you achieve your goal? For what lifestyle are you ready? Can you picture or imagine yourself after you have achieved your goal?

- What specific evidence will you have when you achieve your goal?

- When you achieve your goal, what will be the impact on other aspects of your life? What benefits will you and those around you experience?

- Thinking back, what roadblocks got in the way of your ability to accomplish your goal? What has held you back from experiencing success? (Include thoughts, feelings, emotions, limiting beliefs, paradigms, resentments, and anything else that has held you back.) How can you now better manage these roadblocks?

- What resources do you need to accomplish this goal and what action steps will you take?

- In order to accomplish your goal, how do you need to feel and think on a consistent, daily basis? What can you do to feel and think this way? What can you change so that you will have a new and rewarding experience?

After a period of focused intention, we need to evaluate our efforts and ask if we are reaching our goals, if we need to change our strategies, if we need additional resources, or if we really want to address a particular goal at this time. I did not want to list all of the topics and questions we typically discuss in coaching sessions, but I wanted to share the ones that speak to the part of the process that we frequently neglect. From these questions alone, I hope that we will all stop thinking that there are quick fixes. In the *Emotional Intelligence 2.0*[3] workshop and training I facilitate using TalentSmart's program, we encourage participants to work on only one goal per month. Any quick fix—just decide, just do, just believe, just have faith—typically will not sustain the godly changes we seek or result in the holiness we're called to. Change is a process that starts with a decision. Let's learn even more about this process! Two more change models are presented in Appendix III.

REFLECTION:

Have you consistently focused on understanding your behavior and developing motivation for change? For your personal goals, have you considered the above questions?

Church Success

There are numerous helpful resources that discuss the change process. Dr. Jay E. Adams is well known among Christian counselors, as he has written over fifty books including works on pastoral ministry, counseling, Bible study, and Christian living. In *How to Help People Change: The Four-Step Biblical Process,* Adams shares that he has "witnessed a profusion of well-meaning but ill-taught pastors and Christian workers attempting to unsuccessfully help others to change."[4] He was encouraged by the Christians' willingness to help others, yet he states that, "try as they may, many run smack up against the hard realities, only to discover that their best intentions are no substitute for knowledge and skills. Though sincerely wanting to see change, they simply do not know how to bring it about. In order to help others, they first need help in understanding the counseling process itself."[5] He notes that when helpers (mentors or disciplers) are not biblically directed or do not have the necessary training, we can do more harm than good. We can give bad advice which can lead to harmful action. Most telling is his statement that as helpers, we can leave "the situation unchanged by misdirecting energy, so as to produce more problems rather than solutions."[6] I typically refer participants in the *Healing for Damaged Emotions Workbook* discussion groups to licensed professionals. Since many of us have damaged emotions and wounds from trauma, it makes no sense to me to attempt to put Band-Aids on these problems rather than to attack them with the best resources that are available.

I also must note that there are a number of disciples who have been very successful at helping people change. Perhaps you have given or received that kind of help. Amen! There are also disciples who have had some training in counseling. I just want to caution that just as one with cancer would not want to entrust themselves to a person who is not a licensed and board-certified oncologist, I strongly encourage disciples to find licensed social workers, psychologists, and psychiatrists for the most effective and efficient means for personal growth.

I read Adam's *How to Help People Change* and am delighted to say that our churches have done a wonderful job helping us to understand and attempt to apply 2 Timothy 3:14–17, from which Adams derives his four-step process:

> But as for you, continue in what you have learned and have become convinced of, because you know those from whom you learned it, and how from infancy you have known the Holy Scriptures, which are able to make you wise for salvation through faith in Christ Jesus. All Scripture is God-breathed and is useful for teaching, rebuking, correcting and training in righteousness, so that the servant of God may be thoroughly equipped for every good work.

Adams breaks down his biblical four-step process (teaching, conviction, correction, and disciplined training in righteousness) so that we can all work toward changes that honor God and help others. Our leaders have done a great job teaching us most of what Adams communicates in his book regarding this process of change that he believes "goes beyond minimal or incidental modifications in a person's behavior."[7] He notes that the goal is to use God's word and rely on the Holy Spirit to alter our heart for substantial change in our relationships with God and others. He also remarks that "sanctification, change toward God, is the goal of all Christian counseling."[8] "Pasting on" discipleship behaviors will not create substantial change and thus will not bring glory to God. Without an effective process, a systematic series of actions directed toward some end, we choose to be like the foolish versus the wise builder in Luke 6: 46–49:

> "*Why* do you call me, 'Lord, Lord,' and do not do what I say? As for everyone who comes to me and hears my words and puts them into practice, I will show you what they are like. They are like a man building a house, who dug down deep and laid the foundation on rock. When a flood came, the torrent struck that house but could not shake it, because it was well built. But the one who hears my words and does not put them into practice is like a man who built a house on the ground

without a foundation. The moment the torrent struck that house, it collapsed and its destruction was complete" (emphasis added).

Let's figure out why we are stuck. Let's figure out *why* we think and behave as we do. This understanding will enable us to build well. Let's be wise in how we attack our lifetraps and help each other to do the same!

REFLECTION:

How have you seen zeal without knowledge (Proverbs 19:2) do more harm than good when it comes to advice about heart and soul issues?

_____

_____

_____

Have you ever attempted to shortcut the sanctification and growth process by pasting on discipleship behaviors? How did that work for you in the long run?

_____

_____

_____

Is It Working for You?

I absolutely love Dr. Phil's common question to people who come on his show seeking his assistance. When guests have continued in behaviors that have not gotten them the result they desire, but they are not open to additional suggestions, he often asks, "How's that working for you?" As I've said, another of my all-time favorite quotes is: "Insanity is doing the same thing over and over again but expecting different results." In the Basic Text of Narcotics Anonymous we can also find a similar statement: "Insanity is repeating the same mistakes and expecting different results."

I am so very proud of my mom who at seventy years old decided to stop doing the same things over and over and expect different results. I am who I am today because of my mom. My passion, compassion, love of learning, tenacity, and positive personality traits are mirrors of all the blessings God has given to my mom. My father even jokingly admitted that everything good we have in our characters, skills, and abilities is because of my mom. My sister Carmen (who is a disciple in Charlotte, North Carolina) and I, on the other hand, love to blame our mom when we notice that we are struggling with some of the same challenges she does. The three of us usually get a great laugh out of our blameshifting attempts.

Mom has shared that what is most helpful for her are the professional counseling sessions where her licensed counselor (a cognitive therapist) guides her through a discussion process where she can get to the roots of her feelings and thoughts. She wanted to work on being more in touch with her emotions, since she had previously attempted to close them off, ignore, and devalue them. She has since learned that emotions always find a way to come out—one way or another. Since we are not just spiritual beings, but also physical, psychological, and social beings, we need to work on all of these areas so that we can be more like Jesus who did everything well.

Changes of this type and depth are difficult to bring about and make permanent. They involve significant psychological effort and constitute real personality growth. We all could stand to be more intentional in these efforts. My hope and prayer is that all disciples can enjoy the fruits of changes in these areas and the benefits of being "born again" emotionally. Jesus was an amazing example of emotional intelligence and maturity. We too can be like him in our hearts and souls!

Related Scriptures for Personal Study

Some time later, Jesus went up to Jerusalem for a feast of the Jews. Now there is in Jerusalem near the Sheep Gate a pool, which in Aramaic is called Bethesda and which is surrounded by five covered colonnades. Here a great number of disabled people used to lie—the blind, the lame, the paralyzed. One who was there had been an invalid for thirty-eight years. When Jesus saw him lying there and learned that he had been in this condition for a long time, he asked him, *"Do you want to get well?"*

"Sir," the invalid replied, "I have no one to help me into the pool when the water is stirred. While I am trying to get in, someone else goes down ahead of me."

Then Jesus said to him, "Get up! Pick up your mat and walk." At once the man was cured; he picked up his mat and walked (John 5:1–9, emphasis added).

"Repent [changing one's mind or heart about someone or something], then, and turn to God, so that your sins may be wiped out, that times of refreshing may come from the Lord" (Acts 3:19).

REFLECTION:

What would you do if you weren't afraid?

How would consulting a licensed professional expedite your growth and change your goals?

_____

_____

_____

I will "stop the insanity" and get to heart and soul love by doing the following:

1. _____

2. _____

3. _____

4. _____

This is the last freedom—to choose one's attitude in any given set of circumstances, to choose one's own way. —Victor Frankl

Though there are many more testimonies that could have been included in this book, I pray that you have been inspired by those you read here to allow God to bring about your heart and soul growth goals and turn your tests into testimonies of deliverance and healing.

In closing, please pray through the serenity prayer used in many 12-step groups:

O God and Heavenly Father,
grant to us the serenity of mind
to accept that which cannot be changed,
courage to change that which can be changed,
and wisdom to know the one from the other,
through Jesus Christ our Lord, amen.

Epilogue

Still a Work in Progress—
Prayers Greatly Appreciated!

Writing a book about maturing spiritually is inherently difficult because life continues to provide challenges, and the maturing process never ends. I'm sharing more of my story here because I want my readers to be encouraged that, no matter how trying the circumstances, you can continue to grow spiritually.

Much has happened since I first started writing this book in 2008. The most challenging events included changing school districts where I served as a supervisor for teachers, my father unexpectedly passing in September 2009, both of my grandmothers passing, and retiring and moving south due to medical issues. On top of all of this, dating and a 2008 proposal that did not lead to marriage was incredibly disheartening. Like most young ladies, I had hoped and prayed to be married and have a family. Yet like most of us, I would definitely rather be single and content than to be stuck in an unhealthy or unfulfilling relationship!

I continued seeing a professional therapist through those difficult times. In accordance with her professional duties, my therapist informed me a couple of times that we should close my case and that, even with continued challenges, I was doing just fine. I don't think that I was waiting for the next shoe to drop, but I knew myself well enough to know that I would need informed support during transitions and special situations.

In 2010, after feeling abnormally highly fatigued for a few months, I went to a rheumatologist to get checked out. My father had Addison's disease so I wondered if I had something similar. The rheumatologist ran some tests and determined that I had subclinical Sjogren's disease. There was nothing to treat and nothing serious to be concerned about. Fast-forward a couple of years and the fatigue came back with a vengeance. I found another rheumatologist and he conducted additional tests before sending me to a hematologist for even further testing. Incidentally, he did not tell me that the hematologist was also an oncologist, so I was shocked and scared when I saw the doctor's business card.

The hematologist notified me that I definitely had pre-myeloma, but that a bone marrow test would be needed to make sure that I didn't have multiple myeloma. I gave the bone marrow sample (horrifically painful process) right before the World Discipleship Summit in 2012, and upon my return home to New Jersey, I was informed that I had myeloma, but not multiple myeloma (the most active stage of bone marrow cancer). The word cancer puts fear in just about everybody. This entire process was beyond scary; yet, since there were no debilitating effects at that time, I expected to continue to work.

A few months later, I began to feel even worse. I took myself to the emergency room at the end of September. All types of tests were conducted. I had continued my appointments with the rheumatologist as he went back and forth considering the markers for lupus and fibromyalgia. Finally, in October 2012 he diagnosed me with lupus and fibromyalgia. I was relieved that my cancer was not progressing and that it was "just lupus." But within a week I couldn't make it through a work day. I took a few days off with the hope of getting better. The rheumatologist prescribed two common medications for lupus. My body rejected both. I then started seeing a holistic doctor. I wasn't able to go back to work and the cold Northeast weather impacted the arthritis that sometimes is present with lupus. I felt that I was quarantined to the house in order to stay out of the cold. I was feeling pretty miserable.

Subsequently, in researching disability retirement, I learned that I would not be able to keep up with the cost of living in New Jersey and that both the winter weather and summer pollen were the opposite of helpful. Though I loved the Central Jersey Church of Christ and didn't want to leave, I knew that a move would be best for my health and my finances. God has worked miracles in my transition to Florida. He provided a buyer for my home in New Jersey within one week of placing it on the market. Since I had over ten years of service and contribution to the New Jersey educators' pension system, my application for disability retirement was approved in 2013. I now have a wonderful new church family here at the

Palm Beach Church (www.palmbeachchurch.org)

The cancer hasn't been giving me problems. It's "smoldering" and has not progressed to multiple myeloma. Living with lupus, on the other hand, is vastly different from the life I was accustomed to. Pain and extreme fatigue are fairly common. "Lupus fog" affects the brain, and the fear of kidney and other complications always lurks. After being physically active all my life, having sufficient energy to exercise only about once a week is also troubling. A $70,000 yearly disparity in income is likewise a strain, and retirement at 46 years old is abnormal.

Never a Dull Moment

So you can see why I felt I needed continued professional support! A chronic illnesses, cancer, and not being able to work when you're accustomed to a great salary are all traumatic losses that can either be handled well spiritually and emotionally or they can take a destructive toll. "Never a dull moment" has generally described my life. Since my conviction and philosophy is to be like Jesus in attempting to do things well (Mark 7:37) so that God can be glorified, I have processed all of these challenges and transitions with the help of my licensed counselor here in Florida. With such intense challenges, I am constantly reminded that I am a work in progress and need to continue to grow and face each day focused on God.

In spite of these trials, I am so grateful to be able to share my passion for emotional health and healing with three groups of women here in South Florida. We're reading, working through, and discussing David Seamands' *Healing for Damaged Emotions Workbook*. The first Miami group finishes the book this month and has decided to continue to meet, invite others, and discuss another book. Together, the group participants are making great progress! As David Seamand terms it, we can all become "healed helpers." I feel blessed to be able to continue to learn, grow, and share the things that God has allowed me to process and overcome.

Please pray for my health and continued efforts to help others heal, become all the more healthy, "do all things well," and live lives to the full (John 10:10). I pray that we all will shine like stars—spiritually and emotionally—in this universe and lead many to righteousness!

Those who are wise will *shine like the brightness of the heavens,* and those who lead many to righteousness, like the stars for ever and ever (Daniel 12:3, *emphasis added*).

Therefore, my dear friends, as you have always obeyed—not only in my presence, but now much more in my absence—continue to work out your salvation with fear and trembling, for it is God who works in you to will and to act in order to fulfill his good purpose.

Do everything without grumbling or arguing, so that you may become blameless and pure, "children of God without fault in a warped and crooked generation." Then you will *shine among them like stars in the sky* as you hold firmly to the word of life. And then I will be able to boast on the day of Christ that I did not run or labor in vain. But even if I am being poured out like a drink offering on the sacrifice and service coming from your faith, I am glad and rejoice with all of you. So you too should be glad and rejoice with me. (Philippians 2:12–18, emphasis added).

God's peace.

Chapter Notes

Chapter 1

1. *Matthew Henry's Concise Commentary on the Bible,* http://www.biblestudytools.com/commentaries/matthew-henry-concise/matthew/23.html.

2. Sandra Wilson, *Hurt People Hurt People: Hope and Healing for Yourself and Your Relationships* (Michigan: Discovery House Publishers, 2010), 10, emphasis mine.

3. National Institute of Mental Health, http://www.nimh.nih.gov/health/publications/the-numbers-count-mental-disorders-in-america/index.shtml.

4. The Domestic Violence Resource Center, http://dvrc-or.org/domestic/violence/resources/C61/.

5. Results from the 2008 National Survey on Drug Use and Health: National Findings, Section 3.1. Alcohol Use among Persons Aged 12 or Older, http://www.samhsa.gov/data/nsduh/2k8nsduh/2k8Results.htm#3.1.

6. ChildHelp, http://www.childhelp.org/pages/statistics and McMahon/Ryan Child Advocacy Center http://www.mcmahonryan.org/about-child-abuse/facts-statistics.

7. *THE MESSAGE REMIX* (Colorado Springs, Colorado: NavPress, 2011).

8. Ibid.

Chapter 2

1. Seamands, David A. and Funk, Beth, *Healing for Damaged Emotions Workbook: Recovering from the Memories That Cause Our Pain.* (Colorado: SP Publications, 1992), 217.

2. Ibid., 120.

3. Ibid., 213.

Chapter 3

1. Seamands, David A. and Funk, Beth, *Healing for Damaged Emotions Workbook: Recovering from the Memories That Cause Our Pain.* (Colorado: SP Publications, 1992).

2. Ibid., 205, emphasis mine.

3. Ibid., 207.

4. Comer, Ronald J., *Fundamentals of Abnormal Psychology, Fifth Edition.* (New York: Worth Publishers, 2008), 188.

5. Seamands, 221.

6. Ibid., 78.

Chapter 4

1. Brian Tracy,
http://www.1000advices.com/guru/success_courage_3rules_bt.html.

Chapter 5

1. First Principles,
http://www.caicc.net/wp-content/uploads/2012/03/FirstPrinciples_Eng.pdf.

2. Douglas Jacoby, *Shining Like Stars* (Spring, Texas: Illumination Publishers International, 2006).

3. Benedict Fitzgerald and Mel Gibson, *The Passion of Christ* (Icon Productions, 2004).

Chapter 6

1. Ron Clements, John Musker, and Rob Edwards, *The Princess and the Frog* (Walt Disney Animation Studios, 2009); song "Dig a Little Deeper" by Randy Newman.

2. Peter Scazzero, *The Emotionally Healthy Church: A Strategy for Discipleship That Actually Changes Lives* (Grand Rapids, Michigan: Zondervan, 2013).

3. Daniel Goleman, *Emotional Intelligence: Why it can matter more than IQ* (New York: Bantam, 2006), xxii.

4. *Concise Oxford English Dictionary 12th Edition* (Oxford University Press, 2011).

Chapter 7

1. http://www.nationaleatingdisorders.org/get-facts-eating-disorders.

2. http://www.montenido.com/pdf/montenido_statistics.pdf, source: "Rate of Eating Disorders in Kids Keeps Rising," US Department of Health and Human Services (http://www.healthfinder.gov/news/newsstory.aspx?docID=646574, accessed July 18, 2011).

3. http://www.wlns.com/story/23378205/for-obese-kids-weight-loss-can-sometimes-lead-to-eating-disorders.

4. National Drug Control Strategy Data Supplement, http://www.whitehouse.gov/sites/default/files/ondcp/policy-and-research/2013_data_supplement_final2.pdf.

5. http://www.samhsa.gov/data/NSDUH/2k11Results/NSDUHresults2011.htm.

6. http://pubs.niaaa.nih.gov/publications/brochurewomen/women.htm.

7. Ibid.

8. Ibid.

9. http://womenshealth.gov/violence-against-women/am-i-being-abused.

Chapter 8

1. http://thefatherlessgeneration.wordpress.com/statistics/.

2. Ibid.

3. Ibid.

4. Ibid.

5. Ibid.

6. Ibid.

7. Ibid.

8. http://www.dadsworld.com/parenting-statistics/importance-of-fathers.html.

9. Jennifer Roback Morse. "Parents or Prisons." Policy Review, 2003, http://www.hoover.org/publications/policy-review/article/7976.

10. Lehman, Kevin, *What a Difference a Daddy Makes: The Indelible Imprint a Dad Leaves on His Daughter's Life* (New York: Thomas Nelson, 2000), 5.

11. Dr. Janet G. Woititz, http://alcoholism.about.com/cs/adult/a/aa073097.htm.

12. Wright, H. Norman, *A Dad-Shaped Hole in My Heart: How God Wants to Heal the Wounds Left by Your Earthly Father* (Minneapolis, Minnesota: Bethany House Publishers, 2005), 13.

13. Ibid., 139.

14. Ibid., 144.

15. Ibid., 55.

16. Ibid., 67.

17. http://www.nytimes.com/2008/06/16/us/politics/15cnd-obama.html?pagewanted=print&_r=0.

Chapter 9

1. http://www.thenetworkinc.org/games/leadership-series/mch/.

2. Jeffrey E. Young and Janet S. Klosko, *Reinventing Your Life: The Breakthrough Program to End Negative Behavior...and Feel Great Again* (New York: Plume, 1994).

3. Travis Bradberry and Jean Greave, *Emotional Intelligence 2.0* (San Diego: TalentSmart, 2009).

4. Jay E. Adams, *How to Help People Change: The Four-Step Biblical Process* (Grand Rapids, Michigan: Zondervan, 2010), vii.

5. Ibid., vii.

6. Ibid., viii.

7. Ibid., xii.

8. Ibid., xiii.

Appendix I

Mental Health Disorders

We can be emotionally healthy in spite of a mental health disorder. How we live, deal with, accept, and embrace our challenges makes all the difference. As Christians we rely on God. In 2 Corinthians 12:10, Paul noted: "That is why, for Christ's sake, I delight in weaknesses, in insults, in hardships, in persecutions, in difficulties. For when I am weak, then I am strong". Matthew 8:17 states that "He Himself took our infirmities" (NASB). In addition, Romans 8:26–27 (KJV) promises that the Spirit helps our infirmities and intercedes for us according to the will of God.

It is also our responsibility to utilize medical services. Christians can and should take advantage of the tremendous advances that have been made in psychological sciences, especially since mental health disorders can impact our spirituality. It is imperative for those with mental health disorders to focus on the root, or etiology, of the disorder (biological, social, emotional, neurological, cognitive, etc.) so that those issues can be effectively addressed. **Misdiagnosing a mental health issue as a spiritual issue (pride, selfishness, or laziness, for example) is extremely harmful.** We know that praying and reading our Bibles does not adjust the level of insulin in a person with diabetes, nor will those spiritual disciplines set and heal a broken bone. Spiritual remedies and disciplines for biological or neurological issues will not remedy a mental health disorder. Just as we willingly use the services of oncologists to manage cancer, podiatrists to manage problems with our feet, and ophthalmologists to manage issues with our eyes, **it is immeasurably important that we use the services of psychologists and psychiatrists to manage mental health issues.** Outside of referring individuals to professionals, Christians without professional training in fields of psychology should not attempt to diagnose, analyze, or advise others regarding mental health disorders. We should support each other in our efforts to follow doctors' orders and learn as much as we can about such infirmities. Far too many folks have been erroneously advised not to take doctor-prescribed medicines. Our ignorance in sharing our ill-informed opinions can have spiritually and physically lethal effects.

We all should attempt to learn more, as mental health disorders are highly prevalent in our world. The fifth edition of the *Diagnostic and Statistical Manual of Mental Disorders (DSM-5)* is the official diagnostic system used by mental health professionals to classify and diagnose disorders. The most prevalent US diagnoses are anxiety, mood, and substance abuse disorders. Approximately 20%, 1 in 5, of Americans have anxiety disorders which include phobias, social anxiety disorder, panic disorder, generalized anxiety disorder, and others. Approximately 10% of Americans have mood disorders such as depression and bipolar disorder that are often associated with suicide. "On average, every 20 minutes someone in the US dies from suicide" (Kring, p. 165). At least 60% of those with anxiety disorders will experience depression and vice versa (Kring, p. 135). Substance use and abuse disorders are highly prevalent, with almost 4% of people reporting issues. Substance-related and addictive disorders include problems with alcohol, caffeine, cannabis, hallucinogens, inhalants, opioids, sedatives, stimulants, tobacco, and gambling. Thus, with such high prevalence, as we seek and save the lost and love each other in our fellowships, understanding these disorders and challenges is imperative. We can be emotionally healthy in spite of a mental health disorder. Let's use the professional therapists and psychiatrists whom God has equipped!

Sources cited

American Psychiatric Association, *Diagnostic and Statistical Manual of Mental Disorders, 5th ed.* (Arlington, Virginia: American Psychiatric Publishing, 2013).

Ann M. Kring, Sheri Johnson, Gerald C. Davison, John M. Neale, *Abnormal Psychology 12th Edition: DSM-5* Update (Hoboken, New Jersey: Wiley, 2013).

Appendix II

When to See a Professional Counselor, Psychologist, or Psychiatrist

Many people who want to lose weight see a professional trainer and a nutritionist. Many who want to buy a house use a real estate professional. Those who would like to upgrade their bathroom or kitchen use the services of a contractor. For those who want to effectively and efficiently manage mental health disorders or reduce the impact of emotional health issues, a professional can make all the difference.

In addition, there are times when it is imperative to seek a mental health professional. If you or one of your loved ones experiences any of the following, please seek professional assistance:

1. Significant or prolonged impairment or distress in daily functioning, interpersonal relationships, work, school, sleep, or self-care

2. Self-harm or suicidal thoughts

3. Panic attacks, hallucinations, or delusions

4. Easily irritated or angry

5. No longer have desire for things that previously interested you

6. Past or present sexual, physical, or emotional abuse

7. Seeking relief often from alcohol, cigarettes, or recreational drugs

8. Indulgence in destructive behavior to escape, such as binge eating, shopping, cutting, or pornography

9. Friends express concern about your moods or behaviors

10. God's word and prayers do not help you feel better

11. Your ministry leader does not know how to help you

12. You have struggled with the same sin for years and feel powerless to change

13. Experienced or witnessed a traumatic event and compulsively relive it in your head

Please note that the previous list is not exhaustive.

Any of the following *Disorders found in the Diagnostic and Statistical Manual of Mental Disorders 5th Edition (DSM-5)* should also be addressed with a professional:

- Neurodevelopmental Disorders
- Schizophrenia Spectrum and Other Psychotic Disorders
- Bipolar and Related Disorders
- Depressive Disorders
- Anxiety Disorders
- Obsessive-Compulsive and Related Disorders
- Trauma- and Stressor-Related Disorders
- Dissociative Disorders, Paraphilic Disorders
- Somatic Symptom and Related Disorders
- Feeding and Eating Disorders
- Elimination Disorders
- Sexual Dysfunctions
- Gender Dysphoria
- Disruptive, Impulse-Control, and Conduct Disorders
- Substance-Related and Addictive Disorders
- Neurocognitive Disorders
- Personality Disorders
- Medication-Induced Movement Disorders and Other Adverse Effects of Medication

Source cited

American Psychiatric Association, *Diagnostic and Statistical Manual of Mental Disorders,* 5th ed. (Arlington, Virginia: American Psychiatric Publishing, 2013).

Appendix III

Additional Change Models

Change is a process, not an event. It is a highly personal experience and entails developmental growth in feelings and skills. Change takes time and persistence. The following is a summary of the stages of change from a concerns-based approach. For any area where we'd like to see growth, we can work through such a process in order to reach and sustain our desired outcomes.

Stages of Change: A Concerns-Based Approach

1. **Awareness.** Where people are present-oriented and may not be concerned about change and are not taking action. Individuals are not likely to see opportunities for changes. Information is needed to develop interest in going beyond routine and mechanistic living.

2. **Preparation/planning.** Where one has information about change and how to use the information. People may worry about the impact of change and need support in developing new skills.

3. **Practice/action.** Where one is focused on learning how to think and do things differently. People may be concerned about performance and need support to help solve problems and master new approaches.

4. **Mastery/integration.** Where one is comfortable with the new practices that are integrated into their daily lives. People intentionally look for ways to increase knowledge and skills. Individuals see changes as an improvement and are enthusiastic about the benefits of change. Encouragement is needed in the process along with conversations with others who are changing.

5. **Renewal.** Where individuals plan and work towards improved outcomes and seek effective and innovative alternatives. Information or current data is needed to help in planning and sustaining new ways of living.

Hall and Loucks, *Implementing Innovations in Schools: A Concerns-Based Approach* (Austin, Texas: University of Texas, 1979).

Another representation of the stages of change process, the transtheoretical model, describes stages of change; concerns or areas of focus; issues to address, and tasks to achieve at the respective stages. For our desired areas of growth, working through these steps, thinking through the concerns, considering the issues, and planning to achieve the tasks can move us toward our change goals.

Transtheorectical Model of Change

Stage	Concern	Issues	Tasks
Precontemplation	Need to change	• Denial • Reluctance • Resistance	• Increase awareness of need to change • Increase concern • Envision possibility of change
Contemplation	• Willingness • Readiness • Ability	• More cons than pros • Ambivalence • Fear consequences of change	• Maintain optimum level of anxiety • Patience • Analyze pros & cons
Preparation/ Determination	What will it take?	• Hope for change • Commitment • Plan	• Instill hope • Reinforce commitment • Develop plan
Action	How will it work?	• Success mindset • Efficacy	• Implement strategies • Revise plan • Sustain commitment
Maintenance	Will it continue?	• Sustainability	• Relapse plan • Sustain commitment

James O. Prochaska and Wayne F. Velicer, "The Transtheoretical Model of Health Behavior Change," *American Journal of Health Promotion,* September/October 1997, Vol. 12, No. 1, 38–48.

CPSIA information can be obtained
at www.ICGtesting.com
Printed in the USA
FFOW05n0234100914

9 781941 988978